A GOOD COMPANY WIFE

A GOOD COMPANY WIFE:

My Stories from the Third World

Carol E. Klink

Sacred Life Publishers™
www.SacredLife.com
United States of America

A Good Company Wife:
My Stories from the Third World

Copyright © 2010

All rights reserved. No part of this book may be used or reproduced by any means, graphic, electronic, or mechanical, including photocopying, recording, taping, or by any information storage retrieval system without the written permission of the author except in the case of brief quotations embodied in critical articles and reviews.

A Good Company Wife: My Stories From the Third World may be purchased or ordered through local booksellers, online, or at www.SacredLife.com and www.CarolKlink.com.

ISBN: 0-972-8592-3-3
ISBN: 978-0-9728592-3-3
Library of Congress Control Number: 2010926245

Cover and text design: David Wollangk – Wollangk Design, Inc.
Cover Painting: Carol Klink
Line Drawings: Carol Klink

Sacred Life Publishers™
www.SacredLife.com
Printed in the United States of America

DEDICATION

I dedicate this book to my mother, Daisy Wollangk, who passed away in 1989, but whose presence remains with me always.

I would also like to thank my dear friends, Edna and Walter Van Haerlem who played a huge part in the stories I had to tell.

This book would not have been written without the encouragement of my niece Jill Haberman, and my friend Sharon Lund, PhD, who guided me through the maze.

Lastly, special thanks for her support to my dearest friend Carole Binford who understands me better than anyone, being joined at the hip as we are.

CONTENTS

Introduction xi

Pandora, Costa Rica, 1969–1971 1
Move to Estrella Valley, First earthquake, Horse-biting spider, Parents visit, Scorpion story, Train ride to Limon, Shopping in Limon, Life in Pandora, Learning Spanish, Making bread, Bringing home the eggs, The "library," Becoming a teacher, Marching ants story, The bridge story, Malaria spray program, The Bug Lady, Stealing my neighbor's plant, Playa Cauita, Johannes' plane crash, The big flood of 1970, Moving to Limon.

Limon, Costa Rica, 1971–1973 27
Our new home, Edna's soup, Fanita and Cleo, The giant omelet, Foot card game, Train ride to San Jose, Amoeba, Trip to Panama City, Family visit from Holland, More family from the States, Teaching at the International School, Trip on banana boat to Gulfport, Home robbery, Earthquake in Nicaragua, The Halloween party, Packing for our move.

Davao City, The Philippines, 1973–1977 47
The long journey, The long wait, New maids, New cats, My Minica, Filipino language, Hula, Learning mah jong, Women's auxiliary charity group, Picnic Island, Edna and Walter's arrival, Shelling, Disappearing island, Life in the "boondocks," Weaving, Sewing, Starting a cottage industry business, Kalsangi, The hat story, Flying a plane, Curfew, Trip to Baggio, "It's a Small World," Our trip home, Locked out of my house, Earthquake, News of our transfer, Living at the guest house, Batik mania, The transfer, High school newspaper.

Hua Hin, Thailand, 1977–1987 71

Arrival in Hua Hin, Our house, Bat colony, Cat disappears, Cat fight, New maid, Boonyen's first test, The temples, Fortune told, Shopping by bike, Hua Hin market, Mangos and sticky rice, Managing the cooking, Orange marmalade, Learning Thai, Reading my first Thai word, Shooting elephants, Batiking, Trip to Indonesia, Finding batik dyes in Bangkok, Starting a batik business, Plastic surgery, The barium story, Taking visitors to klong jar factories, The fake antique industry, King's summer palace, Bangkok floating market, "Charie's Brown" restaurant, The wasp nest, Presenting flowers to the queen, Journey to Burma, Barge ride on the Mandalay River, Inlay Lake festival, Rest stop on the lake, Burmese market, Wonderful taxi ride, More shopping, Chiang Mai and the Golden Triangle, Tribal wedding, Riding an elephant, Craft industries, Jill's visit, Sleeping Lion Island, To Chiang Mai on the train, Buying new furniture, Moving to a new house, Creating a new garden, Magpie bird, Peeling a snake, Locked out, Ant swarm, The bird cage, The "took-gae," Home robbery, Songkran, Loy Kratong, Beef tasting party, Company parties at clubhouse, Tak-raw, Thai music, Craft classes, Building a new loom, Learning to haggle in Bangkok, Sam Paeng Lane, Bangkok Buddist market, Jewelry shopping, Look-see trip to Santo Domingo, The long wait, Carving dolls, Packing the house, The trip to Santo Domingo, Losing the cat in Schiphol, Panic in New York.

Santo Domingo, Dominican Republic, 1987–1994 119

Our arrival, Locating a house, "Apagones," Clearing customs, The power bill, Getting water to the house, New maid, Local vegetable market, Getting a driver's license, Grocery shortages, Gas shortages, Tuesday sewing tea, Mah jong group, TV reception, Meeting a new friend Carole, Painting obsession, Learning stained glass, Gisela and pregnancy, Eladia comes to work, Moving to new house, The big "M," Another snake story, Attempted robbery, The Florida health spa, The Ann Wigmore Institute in Puerto Rico, Weekend trip to San Juan, More parakeets, A Special canary, Journey to an island by Honduras, Playing with dolphins, The trip home, Whale watching, Scary close call, Educating our "girls," Our exit from Santo Domingo.

San Jose, Costa Rica, 1994–1996 147

Another move across the world, My 21 year old cat, Looking for an apartment, Central market, Fabric stores on Avenida Central, Parking your car, Being "street smart," Reuniting with old friends, The Victorian sewing box, Craft classes begin, Molding leather, New sculpting passion, "Just a pile of wood," Adopting new birds, The worst day of my life, Going into the rain forest, Elevated cable car through the canopy, Arenal volcano, "Pejibaya" season, The mah jong group, A good Samaritan, A visit from Pom, The accident, News of our transfer, Our farewell party, The departure.

Davao City, The Philippines, 1996–1998 171

Our journey to Davao, New car, Chinatown and market revisited, Receiving our household goods, Our house, Fighting cocks, My new baby, Geni chases birds, Hiring Evelyn, Charity work, Stuffed animals, Jeanne's arrival, English smocking, Community choir, Picnic Island, Computer class, Looking for place to retire, The "gong" incident, Vacation in Vegas, Johannes quits, Our final days abroad.

Epilogue 187

About the Author 189

INTRODUCTION

I was born Carol Eve Wollangk in a small town in Wisconsin. Graduating from Kaukauna High School in 1960, I worked for a while before attending the University of Wisconsin in Madison, majoring in Related Art/Interior Design.

Perhaps because of the rather unusual path I chose to follow since leaving Wisconsin, I have been badgered, prodded, nagged and pestered that "You should write a book," and I am tired of hearing it. These individuals have <u>no idea</u> what they are asking of me. I would wager that even my own family does not have a clue.

I was the third of five children, born of a mother who delighted in words. She played with them, wrote stories, poems, gave oral readings, did crossword puzzles, took creative writing classes, and in general she loved words. Her first two children followed faithfully in her steps. Perhaps she encouraged them in this endeavor, I don't know. That's their story. Then I appeared on the scene, and those genes seem to have been fully spent or maybe her time was much more limited.

There was also another important aspect that I will admit to, since, at my advanced age of 68, I am now long removed from the scene and it really doesn't matter who knows. When I was young, I generally rebelled against anything that smacked of competition, and I surely was NOT going to compete with my two older siblings – if they were going to be readers and writers, I wasn't going there. All through my years of school, all the way through high school, I read as little as possible. Writing essays was the worst and more likely than not, as I sat struggling with yet another two page assignment, Mom would come over and say, "Let me see it," and she would proceed to write the whole thing, or most of it. Of course, it would earn an A+ when I turned it in. But that only compounded the problem, adding guilt to my pile of garbage that I had to drag around with me for the rest of my life.

So now, in this newly realized freedom of senior citizenship, I am cleaning up old unneeded trash, trying to remove the shackles and put a spring in my step. I have decided that I am going to write a book too, since I now know that I don't have to compete with anyone but myself. Mom would be so proud.

This is a book of stories from my life in the Third World. It all happened because of my huge yearning to see the world. I specifically dated only foreign men, knowing that by marrying someone from over the pond, I would have the opportunity to travel. In fact, it would be automatic. And that is indeed what happened. I married Johannes W. Klink from Holland in 1968, and since he was not allowed to remain in the United States to work after he completed his PhD in 1968 at the University of Wisconsin, he accepted a job in Costa Rica with Dole to do research on diseases of bananas and pineapples.

Johannes' new job began as head of research in Costa Rica, which required that he travel between farms around the eastern side of the country. It did not take long for his job to expand to regional head of research and that meant he had to travel also to Nicaragua, Honduras and sometimes to Ecuador where the company had plantations. In future years his horizons were widened even further when we were transferred to the Philippines where he would work for all company operations in

Introduction

the Far East, traveling between the Philippines, Thailand and even China.

But he seemed to thrive in the work since he grew up on a farm in Holland and loved to "get his hands dirty" in the soil. Sleeping on lumpy beds in guest houses and eating at primitive roadside restaurants was all taken in stride and never a complaint. He was taking his many years of education and applying it directly, and this yielded huge rewards to him.

I viewed my roll in his job as "backup." Everyone who climbs a mountain needs a base camp crew, and I was that. It was my job to see that my man's needs were taken care of and he could rest in a comfortable place when he got home. If I had maids to do the actual cleaning and cooking, well, then I was a "manager" of the household and that counted too. These were all beliefs that I cultivated over the years, and Johannes was well aware of their value.

So in that eventful year of 1969, we packed our two bags and headed south to a banana plantation on the east coast of Costa Rica, moving into a company housing compound named Pandora, and our 30 years with the Dole Foods Company began. Come with me now through fears, tears and self-discovery, but also many laughs along the way on my journey into the Third World.

PANDORA, COSTA RICA
1969–1971

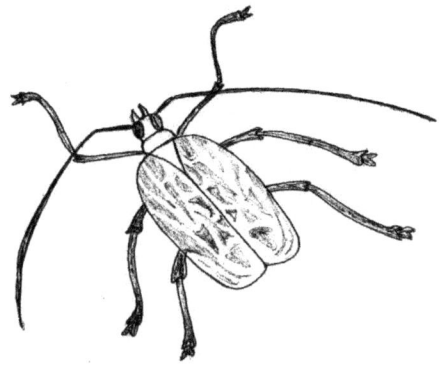

Pandora, Costa Rica

My life took a 180 degree turn at that moment of stepping off the plane. And what an adventure it was! First off, a hurricane hit Gulf Port, Mississippi, the day before our flight, so we had to spend our first night in Memphis. The next day we were able to continue on to New Orleans, and then to San Jose, the capitol city of Costa Rica. A third flight brought us to Limon, a port city on the Caribbean Sea. I looked down as we were approaching and saw only sand and sea. Were we going to land on the beach? The DC-3 plane's wheels touched ground before I could see anything resembling a landing strip. The "terminal" was an unpainted shack with a wind sock on top, but there was no lighting whatsoever and any plane coming in after 6pm had to be shown the way by lining up a few cars by the landing strip and turning on their headlights. The next day a smaller four seat plane flew us into Estrella Valley and the banana plantation which would be our home.

I was suddenly a lady of leisure with nothing to do in the middle of that jungle, but the beauty of the place astounded me. I began to write letters home, ten pages in length, every day, to try to convey to my family what I was seeing out my front window.

The house given to us was the newest one built and was surrounded on three sides by virgin forest, so dense that you would need a machete to slash your way beyond the edge of my "yard." And I had absolutely no desire to do that, what with the long list of deadly snakes and critters that lived there. Not a day passed that the community yardman would not cross my yard with a dead snake hanging over his machete – good eating, you know. So I was very content to stay on the road.

Each morning I would hear this unusual barking sound, and I would peer through my window into the dense foliage to try to see something. One day I caught a glimpse of movement and looked high up in the trees and saw this spectacular black monkey with a thick white mane around his neck. Soon thereafter I saw the rest of the family, babies hanging onto their mothers as they swung through the trees, headed to the guava tree in my "front yard."

There were noises that I never was able to identify and I had to assume that animals were coming down to the small stream that ran out back of my house. One day I asked Johannes to trim the ends of my long hair since a trip to a beauty salon was not an option for me. We went into the back bedroom which faced the jungle. Suddenly a big iguana, probably 8 feet long, came slithering up very close to the window. Johannes started yelling, "Take a picture! Take a picture." I replied that to take a picture of that animal, which was so camouflaged against the heavy foliage of the jungle, would be worthless since you would never see the animal. But I grabbed the camera anyway and took that photo. Of course, a roll of film would take many months to have processed, so it was perhaps six months before I received the prints from that roll. In looking through the pile, I found this photo of our back yard and wondered why on earth I had taken that picture. Another several months later, during a discussion with someone, the subject of iguanas came up, and it snapped into my mind – ah, the back yard photo. I got the pile of pictures out and, sure enough, you could just see the pale yellow on the under side of the iguana's head.

That house in the jungle was the backdrop to many stories. Since this is a book of my stories, here's another one. I was sitting at our dining room table, the legs of which were a bit askew even though it was brand new, writing yet another long letter home, when suddenly I experienced my first earthquake, the first of many I would have over the years. I felt a nausea and fear that is hard to describe, not knowing what to do in that moment. Fortunately, it was over in a matter of seconds and I stumbled to my feet and went out to my small kitchen where the maid was standing washing the dishes. I said, with the little Spanish I knew at that time, "Did you feel that!?!" She turned and said "What?" It amazed me that a person could become so accustomed to the earth shifting under their feet that they no longer noticed it. I can say that that never happened to me. Every quake produced that same dizzy nausea and fear, but I have a better idea of what to do now, after having experienced so many small tremors.

Sitting at that same table, again writing a letter home, I decided to get up and put something into the garbage pail outside the door of the back patio. This patio had a door with lattice work covering the screen, and I had learned that it was a good idea to bang the door several times before opening it fully to dislodge anything that might be hanging on to it, since you could not see through the lattice. So that day I opened the door slightly and slammed it shut a couple times. The third pull was to open the door fully and as I did that this HUMUNGOUS black hairy spider dropped off the door, missing my shoulder by a fraction. I STARTED RUNNING FOR THE KITCHEN DOOR WITH THE SPIDER CHASING ME, GRABBING THE BROOM ON THE WAY, AND IN ONE VERY LUCKY SWIPE I HIT THE SPIDER, SENDING IT TO THE OTHER SIDE OF THE PATIO. It sat there without moving, perhaps stunned by the hit, and at that moment the yardman came walking into my back yard. I screamed at him to come immediately and he entered the patio and saw the mammoth spider I was pointing at. He continued walking until he was standing in my kitchen door – WITH HIS BACK TO THE SPIDER – and he told me his own experience with this Horse Biting Spider that bit him and his arm was swollen up for six months. (I know that my grasp of the Spanish language at that time may have affected the translation of his words, but that is what I understood him say.) I just wanted him to quit talking and kill the thing, so finally him rather casually turned around and with his long machete, which was never absent from his belt, he stabbed the insect. I returned to the letter I was writing at the dining room table and continued, but there was a decided difference in my handwriting before and after the horse biting spider.

My parents decided to visit us soon after we had moved to Pandora, their first trip out of the United States. My mother, having been born and raised in the woods of northern Wisconsin, was thrilled with the idea of "exploring" my jungle. I had to bring her down and say, "Mom, it's too dangerous to go walking even in my yard, much less through the dense trees surrounding it." And she would reply, "Oh, you sissy!" But I managed to keep her at least on the path. Being so new to the country, I didn't know where or how to go to entertain them, so we just explored what we could of Estrella Valley from the truck, touring through the whole banana operation and around the edges.

Once Johannes brought home a "tip over" stem of bananas. This was from a banana plant that got top heavy and fell over on the road, thus becoming worthless. But it was <u>100 pounds</u> of bananas, and my mother thought we had to somehow eat them all! With the few precious eggs I could find, we made banana breads, banana pie, banana cake, bananas on our morning cereal, and in between we ate bananas for snacks. Still we couldn't eat 100 pounds and some, alas, had to be tossed.

I know you may tire of my bug stories by the time I finish writing this book, but I can't leave this scenario without relating my story about the scorpion. In those first few months of moving from Manhattan, Kansas, to the jungles of Costa Rica, I had gained some weight and decided to see a doctor for help. He prescribed some diuretic pills, with the result that I would have to get up in the middle of the night to pee. Our master bedroom had a tiny bathroom, probably 4' by 5' not including the shower stall, and I did not want to disturb Johannes by turning on the light, so it was my habit to go into the bathroom, close the door and then turn on the light, all the while keeping my eyes closed to avoid the glare. Because the room was so small, I could easily find my way to the toilet without opening my eyes. And that is when I would open them as I sat down. That night was special for when I opened my eyes, there exactly at eye level and about two feet in front of my eyes was a <u>huge</u> black scorpion on the wall (in the jungle all bugs were huge). I immediately lifted my feet off the floor and my movement disturbed the critter and he began to crawl down the wall, across the doorway and over into the corner by the shower. It was a good time to make my escape. I leaped up and ran into the bedroom, but NOW what to do? How could I begin to go to sleep with that thing so close by. Surely it would find its way into my bed! The only thing that came to mind was to capture it and I remembered a large coffee can I had in the kitchen. I quickly found that can and began, fearfully, to creep up behind the scorpion which was still in the corner, and I plopped that can right over it. He was understandably very irritated by this maneuver and began to race around inside, making quite a noise in the process. This made me think that he was probably strong enough to turn the can over and escape, so now the dilemma was how to keep him in the can. I started to back out of the bathroom on my hands and knees, keeping the can firmly attached to the floor and hoping I wasn't awakening Johannes in the process. It seemed a good idea to put something heavy on top of the can, so I found one of Johannes' old heavy work boots and placed it on top. At last, a feeling of relief came over me and I was able to crawl into bed and sleep. But you know what happens when you close your eyes to avoid seeing something unwanted (or put a boot on top of a can), the problem doesn't go away, and sure enough, I had to deal with the situation in the morning. By this time people were beginning to arise and I explained the problem I had. My first thought was to get some spray poison and squirt it under the can, but doing this, I could tell that he was still very much alive. I had no Plan B, but Dear Ol' Dad came to my rescue. He simply picked up that old boot, lifted the can, and with one fluid movement, removed the problem once and for all. My reaction was – why didn't I think of that last night?

A highlight of my parent's trip was a train ride into the closest town, Limon, about a two hour trip on good days. What I mean by that is this passenger train had to defer to the trains hauling bananas because there was only one track. So our train would go off on a side rail and wait, sometimes an hour or more, for the bananas to pass before continuing on our journey through cacao plantations. Along the way there were many stops, being the only means of transportation in and out of the jungle. People would hop on to walk up and down the aisles selling their wears and local goodies to eat, mostly things fried in deep fat. The smells of all that, along with the distinctive stench of the cacao husks being burned to make charcoal along the way, will remain with me forever.

We sat on wooden seats and all the windows were open, being hot and humid as it was, and the train would rock you back and forth, clickity-clacking down the rails. Mom even wrote a poem later about this, I believe. I think she found it very exotic, what with all the wild orchids hanging from trees and philodendrons wrapped around any upright stick. It was surely a gardener's paradise. If you stuck a bare stick into the ground, it

Pandora, Costa Rica

would begin to sprout in short time, due to the 250 inches of rain annually.

It was not always fun to take this trip, however. In fact, I grew to dread it and would only schedule the run for when I ran out of dish washing liquid. Yes, that was it, my life revolved around dish washing liquid. The journey would begin by a telephone call (using a crank phone) to the local operator who would call to a small "colmado" (grocery store) at the foot of our hill. This place can only be described as a decrepit shack with old canned foods that were rusted and dusty up on the shelves along with rats that ran around in the rafters. There were some tables set up if you wanted to sit and have a drink, but I never felt inclined to do that. My sole objective was to wait for the train which would stop there because a red flag had been hung outside to signal a passenger was waiting. Because this was the last stop at the end of the valley, most all the seats were taken and at times I had to stand for a while, trying not to fall over as the train swayed back and forth.

Limon was more of a town than city, and the population was mostly black people who were the descendents of Jamaicans brought in to build the railroads. Until, I think, the 1950's, they were not allowed to leave the Atlantic Zone, and so they had settled in Limon and they spoke an interesting dialect of English. As my Spanish at that time was very sketchy, it came in handy a few times to be able to communicate in my own tongue. I remember one time when I wanted to find molasses and had no idea of the Spanish term and was completely unable to get the idea across to the shopkeeper. A large black woman came by and saved the day and told me, "You have to <u>burn</u> your own molasses here" using a cake of raw brown sugar.

1969–1971

Such was grocery shopping in that port city. The Limon market was my first Third World experience with an open market, and nothing has fazed me since. The area was very dirty, hot, of course humid, muddy and rats and flies everywhere. There was an attempt to screen in the meat stall, but it was a half hearted attempt at best. The stall had many carcasses hanging there and you would (in my case) point to the area you wanted to buy. The butcher would take a large machete – what else? – and hack off that particular area, and I would call it a chuck roast. No matter how you prepared the meat, it was always tough and "gamy," so I would beat it with a mallet before any cooking and lay strips of papaya on the meat to help tenderize it. These were all tricks that I was learning from my local neighbors.

A problem that I had to surmount on my shopping day was what to do between the time I finished shopping and the return train at 3pm in the afternoon. I would be loaded down with bags of groceries which I could stash at the company office near the train station, but then I had to occupy myself for those several hours. In the beginning I would buy some lunch and take it to a little park right there in front of the office and on the ocean. It was a pleasant place with lots of benches and giant sloth animals up in the trees which were hard to spot because they moved so slowly. Then my walks in the park came to a screeching halt and I learned it was a dangerous place for a single, foreign woman to be sitting all alone. As I sat there that day, a young man came walking by and I noticed him but paid little attention. He remained in the corner of my eye, however, and after several passes in front of me, where he was now making a hissing sound as he walked by, I was now paying close attention to him, and I saw him pick up a rock at the edge of the park. This was all I needed to grab my things and make a run for it. I now believe this little scene was a good lesson to me in "street smarts." Always be aware of your surroundings, especially if you are a lone foreign woman on the street. You <u>will</u> be a target.

When you live in a tiny community like Pandora with about 30 homes, built by the company for the executives, as a non-working wife, you got to know everyone quite well. There was really no place to go for entertainment, no stores or movie theaters, no cars to get there anyway for the women, just a gravel road down the center with a couple branches along the way. That was it. So we depended on one another for entertainment. This meant that women would gather most every day at a centrally located home and we would drink tea and eat cookies and talk while the smaller children played around the room. And the talk would usually revolve around the kids, maids and recipes. Much of the chatter would pass right over my head because my grasp of Spanish was minimal at this point, but this is how I began to learn the language by complete emersion in it. Every now and then someone would face me and loudly ask me something in Spanish. I would stare intently at their lips to try to make out individual words, grasping at straws to make sense out of what they were saying. I was learning on my feet, as they say. At least I did not have to write exams, no?

Another thing I was beginning to learn was cooking. Growing up, mostly my mother or older sister did that, and I had just skimmed along in survival mode by opening cans of this or that. (It could be this was just another form of rebellion.) Now, with that not an option, I had to take up the reins of cooking for my new husband who, I am sure, was thinking a wife's cooking should compare with his mother's. An example of my new adventure was making bread. I could not find any bread at the market that didn't taste very sweet, so using a recipe from my sister, I gave it a try. I had to develop some new muscles for all that kneading, and my first attempts were not great. But gradually eatable results began to emerge from the oven. And so began thirty years of baking all the bread consumed in our household. Later in the game I did acquire a marvelous Cuisinart which made things a bit easier.

Another learning experience was making cakes from scratch. There were a few imported mixes available but they were never successful because, you see, living near the equator and sea level, the leavening was not correct. I was told that I must increase the baking soda by twice in that heavy atmosphere.

And there was one other thing about baking cakes that was a challenge and that was to find the eggs necessary for the recipe. To bring them from Limon on my monthly trip there was difficult to say the least. One time I tried to bring several dozen eggs, and while getting on the return train the bundle slipped from my hands and smashed down the center aisle of the train car. I tried to scrape them aside with my foot, but it was a sorry mess.

My neighbor was raising chickens next door and would offer me eggs sometimes, and now and again I would be able to buy them from a small grocery in the valley, but it was always hit or miss. Then this same neighbor was transferred away and I assumed care of the chicken coop. The eggs were lovely, but the price I paid was to be bitten by fleas every time I went inside the cage to gather the eggs. I was paying in blood for every cake I baked.

Living in this small village with only local Spanish radio (no TV of course), newspaper and conversation, I soon became "starved" for the English language. I discovered that there was a small bookcase down at the clubhouse where visitors would donate their novels and I began to check them out. Most were terrible westerns or science fiction, but it didn't matter – the only criteria was that they were written in English. This was really the first time in my life that I had begun to read books of any kind just for entertainment. What a revelation that I actually enjoyed reading!

One day a company official came to me asking that I take over the tutoring of three kids, first, second and third grades, from another American woman who was leaving. These kids had begun their schooling up in the States and their parents wanted them to continue with English. Thus I began my own education in teaching primary school. It was a correspondence course, so essentially I would read the three different lessons first and keep one jump ahead of each child. Our school was around my increasingly leaning dining room table. Every morning they came around 9 am and left at 11:30. In the afternoons they attended Spanish school.

One day as the four of us were sitting there, Roberto startled me by saying, "WOW, LOOK!" to which I did indeed look at where he was pointing. It was at the base of the front door close by, under which was pouring a sea of large ants. It was a solid black mass of terror! I ran for my handy can of spray poison and some brooms, arming each kid with a weapon. To my dismay, the ants were also coming in my only other outside door in the kitchen, thus cutting off our escape. We began to spray, sweep and try to deter them as best we could, and since I am sitting here writing this, it is obvious that those critters did not swarm over our bodies and devour us, leaving clean white bones on the floor. We managed to divert their march which began from out in the jungle, hit the corner of my house, split ranks and one branch came in under my front door and one the back. Now, because of our frantic efforts, these two branches again met up on the opposite corner of the house and continued their march toward the village.

At this point it became a wonderful science project and we stood by watching the progress of the line. The ants were so dense that they left a trampled path about four inches wide through the grass. Suddenly, as if someone had sounded a trumpet, the ants did an about face and retraced their steps back into the jungle. I never saw them again, and thank God for that.

Around the edges of the valley there were several "independent farmers" who would grow bananas and sell them to the company. One such farm, Vesta, was located across the river at the far end of the valley. It was a treat to have large community picnics out there on Sundays, but I only went once. Here's why. The Bridge Story. (Drum roll.)

We packed our picnic lunches and headed out in a caravan of trucks toward Vesta, about half an hour's drive away. That is the end of the road and there was only this one farm across the river and then it goes into steep mountains and impenetrable forest beyond. There are local Indians that live up there and you would see them once in a while as they came down to the valley to buy supplies. The men would be walking along the road with the women trudging behind carrying on their backs large loads of whatever it was they would sell. The return trip would be the same with the women doing all of the carrying of supplies back to their forest homes.

We parked our vehicles and unloaded our picnics, and it was then that I saw the next step – to get across the river. Since the farm had to get its bananas across the river too, a conveyor belt inside a metal tube had been built that spanned the width. On top of this tube had been placed a 6 inch wide plank for all foot traffic. Then "for stability" two cables had been stretched from shore to shore for you to hang on to during your crossing.

Pandora, Costa Rica

However, when the cable reached the middle of the river, it was about five inches above your ankles, and this whole thing was swaying in the breeze and if more than one person was on the bridge, it bounced up and down. On top of it all, the whole suspension bridge was many, many feet above a shallow, rocky, swiftly moving river below. I took one look and the gripping fear made me pee my pants, no lie. There was no way in HELL that I could go across. At this point I was totally amazed as a man ON A BICYCLE rode across that 6 inch plank. He should have been in the circus with that talent. I was not alone in my fear, so a small boat was rounded up for a few of us women and we reached the far shore.

It was a lovely day and the beer was flowing. I began to get a little nervous as the hours wore on, however, not being a beer drinker myself, and began thinking about that damned thing between me and home. By late afternoon, I started nagging my husband that it was time to go because it would be raining soon, but he was only listening to the beer by then. And so my worst fears were realized. The sun dropped behind the mountains about 6pm, it was pitch black and the rains began. Now it was time to break up the party. Perfect. The boat could not be launched due to the rain, or something, so it was walk that plank or be left behind. It was decided to make the crossings in groups of 3, everyone carrying something, which meant you had only one hand to hang on to that cable. It was so dark and slippery, not to even mention the fact that most of the men had had way too many beers. My group consisted of Gabriela, who had polio as a child and one leg was shorter than the other. She got to carry a small flashlight. I came next carrying a basket of picnic stuff. Then came Johannes who also carried something. I could hear the roar of the river below as we started out with great caution. Soon we had reached about the middle of the expanse, judging from how low the cable was at that point.

Then it happened. Johannes fell, shaking that bridge like a limp rope. Gabriela and I hung on desperately to that cable and I turned around, expecting that Johannes would be smashed on the rocks below. But there he was, hanging on with one leg over that plank. I have no idea how I managed to help him back to his feet, but we all made it across. Maybe you can understand now why I never went to Vesta again.

Let me tell you about the official spray program of Costa Rica at that time. It was a written law that every six months all buildings on the Atlantic side of the country had to be sprayed with DDT against malaria. It did not seem to matter that DDT was banned in the United States as a deadly poison. To their way of thinking, malaria was a larger threat. So this is what would happen. They would call you up and schedule your hour for the crew to arrive. You would prepare for their coming by stripping your walls in every room of everything, all furniture would be placed in the center of the room covered with a tarp, and you would have to cover all the dishes and food inside your cabinets just in case. All houses had the same type of windows which were these "jalousie" slats that you could tilt open or closed with a lever (I spit on the grave of whoever invented them). After my first experience with the spray crew, I tried to cover the windows with newspaper on the outside, hoping to save myself a little work later. This failed miserably because they proceeded to spray the windows from the inside. Their MO was to enter the house with large sprayers filled with gallons of DDT and they would spray EVERYTHING, your walls, ceilings, windows, and it would be so thick that it would run down the walls and make puddles on the floor. We would be asked to leave the house for several hours and were told NOT to wash their spray off when they were finished. It would take a week to get your house back to normal, and then you had to know that you were still living with lots of DDT, even though you had tried to wash everything.

One time we ladies of Pandora decided to stage a protest. They were very concerned for their children, especially the babies. We were all, as a unit, going to not allow any spray man to enter our homes. The day arrived, and one by one, the women fell, and finally it was my turn, being the last house at the end of the last street. The men wearily came to my door and as I looked in their eyes, I knew I was standing alone, so I just opened the door and let them do their thing. United you might stand a chance, divided you surely fall.

It was in Pandora that I became know as The Bug Lady. Before going to the tropics, I lived with two brothers, and Larry was taking a course in entomology at the university there in Madison. He and I would go out to the arboretum to collect various species of insects, and then we would mount them for display. When I moved to Pandora I brought with me the equipment needed to do this. So I began almost immediately to collect some beetles and butterflies which abounded in my yard. I had a large piece of cardboard from a packing crate and used that to display my collection.

As time went by, I had quite a large collection, and people began to call me to say they had a bug in their house and would I come to get it. I would grab my butterfly net and race over, all excited to be adding something new to my display. One day I tried to collect a giant longhorn beetle that was clinging to the back patio door (remember the horse biting spider?). Each antenna measured 8 inches and the body was the size of the back of my hand! It was so large that when I went into my kitchen looking for something to plop over the top of the insect,

1969–1971

I couldn't find anything large enough and feared breaking an antenna. So I went for the spray poison again and sprayed and sprayed. He would just wiggle a bit, but seemed unaffected, and finally he just hauled himself up and flew like a tank back into the jungle. I was so disappointed that I could not collect him, but sometime later I was able to find one, although a bit smaller. Gorgeous insect with markings of a tortoise in red and dark brown colored fuzzy hair. Long thin legs and antennae. He was a prize specimen.

So bugs were a theme that ran throughout my life in the Third World. Sometimes I was excited to find them, but mostly they had their own means to bring me down to their level. Like the time I had a whole row of plantania flowers planted outside across my large and low living room windows. I was watching them closely and could hardly await the time when I would begin to get lovely red blooms. Finally there were many flowers just busting to open probably tomorrow, so I raced out that morning expecting to see a fabulous display, but was greeted by a long row of sticks. Not a leaf, much less flower, in sight. Sometime during the night some insects, who had also probably been watching and waiting for just the right moment, got there first. I think that yard just wanted to be free to be a jungle and not be tamed.

There was one more plant that had caught my eye, but unfortunately it was in the neighbor's yard. A lovely thing with large almost wooden leaves that spiraled around the main stem. I had been eyeing that plant for quite a while, being located, as it was, just where our two driveways met. Then it came to pass that the neighbors were being transferred away from the valley and they were gone for several weeks, although their house had not been emptied yet. I got to thinking about that plant and how great it would look in a pot in my living room, and if I was going to steal it, I better do it before the new neighbors moved in. I picked up my machete to dig it out and, being sure nobody was around, I went out to do the dirty deed. I no sooner got to the end of my driveway than the husband and wife drove up to their house!! And there I was with a machete dangling from my hand and I was going to have to think fast to explain why. I was not good at being a criminal. My timing was wrong.

A party was being planned for a picnic on the beach of Playa Cauita located half way between Pandora and Limon. This beach was reported to be the prettiest place in all of Costa Rica. Since most husbands were game to go with their wives, I began a nagging campaign to get my own husband to attend, and he very reluctantly gave in. A bit of coordination was required to make our journey possible for our group of about 10 people because someone with a vehicle had to meet us on the opposite side of the river at a small village called Penhurst. The trek began with the usual red flag being hung outside the small grocery down by the railroad tracks and we all piled onto the early morning train for the one hour ride. From there we had to slide down a muddy embankment to the river where there was a small dug-out boat which could carry about four people at a time. The river was not too wide at this point, so the several trips required to get us all across didn't take too long. It was then that we saw our transportation to the beach about five miles away – a dump truck! It was better than walking, or at least we thought that at the time. We piled into the back and away we went at maybe 2 miles per hour because there were giant pot holes all along the road. The joke was that we would just bury the 7 months pregnant woman's child along the way if need be (which seemed very funny at the time, but perhaps you had to be there).

Finally it was declared that we had arrived, and the rain began to fall with perfect timing. We found a small boy who was going to lead us to the beach, because we could not as yet see the water. And at long last we did arrive at the "most beautiful spot in all of Costa Rica" and we had to seek shelter under some rubber trees along the beach. We were all pretty much starving by this time so we spread out our picnics and tried to make the best of it. The rain continued, probably waiting maliciously until it was too late to enjoy the beach. Finally nature was declared the winner and we retraced our steps to our luxury means of conveyance and made the 5 mile/one hour trip back to the river. After recrossing and crawling up the muddy slope once again, now we had to wait for the train which was late. The small grocery had such a stench inside that I chose to sit outside on a wooden bench for the duration.

This was yet another lesson to me to never nag my husband to be more adventurous. I left him pretty much alone all through the rest of our marriage as I never had a leg to stand on after that picnic.

Some moments stand out in your mind more than others, and one of those was the day my husband crashed in an airplane. It was a day like most days and Johannes had left early to fly with three other men over to another banana plantation north of us. So there were four men in this small plane, including the pilot and the manager of the division who also had his pilot's license. As they approached the landing strip at the farm, just a patch of grass between the rows of bananas, a light in the cockpit indicated that the landing gear had not opened. They flew low over the tiny airport and someone on the ground confirmed that indeed they had no wheels to land on. The pilot tried shaking the plane and several other maneuvers but nothing worked. So the manager made the decision to fly up to San Jose while they still had gas and where there was a small airport with a grass strip and also a fire engine. They would make their emergency landing, which in plain terms meant they had to belly flop onto the strip. Johannes and the other passenger were told to take off their belts, glasses and watches and put their heads down (I still don't understand exactly why they had to remove their belts). Then the two pilots brought the plane down in a raised nose position, using all their strength to keep the craft from touching the front end down which would have caused them to flip head over tail. The plane obviously was totaled, but everyone walked away uninjured. The manager immediately got another plane and was anxious to get back to work. Johannes, being the good company man that he was, got right back in the saddle, but the other guy called it a day – with good reason I would say.

I had had an uneventful day chatting with the ladies until one husband came home late in the afternoon and said to me, "Your husband certainly had an exciting day!" My eyes must have opened wide and he realized that I knew nothing of events and he would not tell me. I immediately headed up the hill to my house and saw Johannes' pickup in the driveway. Racing in I found him calmly sitting in his chair with the local Spanish newspaper, as if nothing had happened. I had to use a prodding stick to get the story. But in retrospect, I am glad that I did not know the details as they happened and could just find my husband home in one piece.

We spent a total of 18 months living in Pandora and the last few were the most dramatic. It was the great flood of 1970. Beginning sometime in November it began to rain for 40 days and 40 nights, literally a non-stop rain that beat down on our tin roofs without mercy. The whole valley flooded and you could stand at the entrance of Pandora up on a hill and see only water.

It was higher than the banana plants. The 10,000 workers in the fields had to escape to the surrounding hills, the railroad was washed away and the plantation totally destroyed. There was no way to leave because even the grass airport for small company planes was under water. The disaster was of such a magnitude that the American military from Panama had to be called in to drop food to the people in the valley. They brought in large sacks of rice and beans – uncooked, and because there was no way for the locals to cook, they brought those bags up to us ladies in Pandora. They had set up a large generator for our homes on the hill and we were still functioning, so we were pressed into service to cook the rice and beans for the 10,000 people in the valley. I volunteered to do rice, since I had no clue of how to cook beans. In my tiny kitchen I began with all the big pots I could find to boil rice and place it cooked into large plastic bins which were provided for me. I must have had a sticky layer of rice an inch deep on my floor at the end of each day. A truck would come around to collect the bins and distribute them to people. I don't know how.

As days and weeks rolled by with no relief, we executives up on the hill also began to feel pangs of hunger because all the relief efforts by the company and military were directed toward the people in the valley. I guess they assumed we "rich" people up on the hill could eat cake. So we gathered together and let the officials know that we needed some food also. I was more concerned about my maid who lived outside the valley up in the hills somewhere and was not receiving the goodies like the people in the valley. So I requested some rice and beans for her too. When they delivered our lists, the rice and sugar looked like it had been swept off the floor. I felt bad to give it to my maid, but knew it was better than nothing.

Pandora, Costa Rica

For myself, I was fortunate to have received my weekly shipment of vegetables and meat just before the rains began, and I stretched them out over about two weeks, but then I was out of luck too. The water had receded in a few places by then and Johannes came home one evening and announced that he had found some vegetables, some cabbage and potatoes. Yes, they had been floating in water for a couple weeks, but, hey, it was food. The cabbage was muddy to the core and I took each leaf and washed it with soap. Then I began to pare some of the 50 pounds of potatoes and would get perhaps a walnut sized piece that was not rotten. By the time I had pared enough for a meal, I had finished the whole 50 pounds. Johannes sat down that night to what he thought would be one of many days of his favorite Dutch meal, meat, potatoes and cabbage. I told him to enjoy his potatoes because they were the last for a while.

Another service I provided to the community during the flood was a laundromat – I had the only clothes dryer in the village. When you have 100 per cent humidity for 40 days what do you do? I bet you never thought about that. All the homes came equipped with lights at the bottom of each closet to try to stem the mold from growing even under normal conditions. Now those lights got pressed into service to try to dry clothing. The towels never would dry thoroughly. So there was a steady stream of women who lined up at my door every day and my dryer ran constantly. I didn't mind. You just try to do whatever you can to help.

That year in Pandora we had just formed a charity group with the ladies of Pandora and our first project was to raise money to buy a toy for every child in the valley for Christmas. Somehow it was determined there were about 3 or 4 thousand of them and we had a list of ages and sexes. We were going to make a trip out to the capitol city of San Jose to buy the toys when the flood struck and therefore we cancelled the trip but not the plan. As soon as the flood water receded on the air strip, we chartered a small plane to fly us out. Sounds great, no? But this would not be one of my "stories" if it were that simple.

Because so many people had lost their homes, the railroad was washed away, and there was no other way out of the valley, large crowds of people would gather along the grass landing strip trying to get on small, four seat, one prop planes coming into the valley which were carrying executives who had come to look at the damage. The locals would swarm like ants around the plane as it came to a stop and try to be the lucky individual who got a seat. It was chaos.

Christmas was approaching, so we four ladies began our toy run by climbing into the back of a truck which would carry us to the airport. Then as the plane we had chartered came in for a landing we raced toward it, as did the crowd. But we had the upper hand since we were in the truck and were able to fight our way into the plane with the added help of some security people and their elbows. The four seat plane now had five people in it and more were trying to force their way in, but the pilot took his foot and pushed the person out who was already half way into the plane, and slammed the door. He immediately revved up his motor and we took off, parting the crowd like the Red Sea. We barely missed the tops of the banana plants surrounding the airstrip. The rain began again and you couldn't even see the tips of the wings. I think I prayed that day and held on to a locket with a picture of Johannes inside. I figured if we go down, at least anyone finding my body would know to whom I belonged.

We ladies spent a couple days to accomplish all the buying for those children and I was thankful that the group had decided not to wrap each one of those 4000 toys. Our return trip to the valley was nearly as traumatic as the departure, I having picked up a case of "Costa Rican crud" along the way. And, of course, there was the uncertainty of just how we would be able to return home, what with the rain still falling. But we survived it all and then climbed into pickup trucks to visit all the villages in the valley, at least those where the water had receded, and distributed the Christmas presents.

Our days of living in Pandora were limited now as the whole research office was being moved to the port city of Limon. I would miss our small community and the ladies with whom I made bonds that would last a lifetime.

LIMON, COSTA RICA
1971–1973

Limon, Costa Rica

At last our house in Limon, which was being built for us, was ready to be occupied. When the floods in Estrella Valley had receded, I was able to fly out to oversee the building of the house. You know, did I want a closet here or not and where should they put the cabinets in the kitchen? It was very exciting to be involved in the designing of my own place – interior design having been my major at the university years back – so I spent hours pouring over architectural plans. The house was two stories with the car port, maid's quarters and laundry room below and three bedrooms, two baths, the kitchen and living room/dining room combination above. There was a nice front veranda facing the ocean.

This house was the newest one built in the company compound and was placed way back on this hill just north of the town. The chief engineer in charge of housing was a man from the deserts of Arizona, so his idea of beauty was to have wide open vistas. He decided that every house should have a "view of the ocean" so with each new addition (since his arrival) the land was totally cleared of any trees that might obstruct the view. He wanted to start with bare clay. By the time my house was built, it was so far back into the forest that my view was a far distant skyline, with, of course, no trees to obstruct it. I had red clay everywhere and the little tuffs of grass that were plugged into my yard, about two feet apart from each other, never did grow together in the time I was there. But I did have a lovely view of the surrounding forest and it was always a delight to spot an orchid up in a tree or just enjoy a balmy breeze out on my veranda.

No sooner did I get settled than yet another house began to be constructed behind me. A couple, who were coming from Ecuador to live there, already were living temporarily in an old house down by the water and I soon became acquainted with

Edna and Walter. She invited me down for her homemade soup one day and I don't think I ever told her this story. I was being polite. I remember entering the tiny house and smelling this wonderful aroma of her vegetable soup. We chatted a bit and sat down for lunch. I started eating the soup, enjoying it thoroughly, until half way through I looked more closely and saw that the black flecks that I thought were some sort of spice were actually little beetles. This was a very common thing in the tropics that your spices would get bugs, and I didn't know Edna well enough to tell her about it, so I just continued to eat my soup, although trying to eat between the "flecks of pepper."

Since Edna and Walter were overseeing the construction of their new house behind me, they would come up every day for a while and soon got to know a wild cat which had taken up residence in their "bajo" (lower area of the house). They named the cat Fanita, short for Orphanita, and put food out every day for her. I also was feeding the cat so she would come over to my house too. One day I went down to put out new food and I saw another cat in among some large packing crates left from my move. She very aggressively hissed at me and in general indicated that she wanted me to back off. I set the food down and let her eat. I decided that she would be my cat and the next day when I brought food, I sat down on the cement floor and began to talk to her. I named her Cleo right away and I told her how beautiful she was and that it was OK for her to stay, etc. It was soon revealed that she had three kittens stashed in the crates. But that was OK too with me, being a cat person. So each morning for several days I would sit there and talk to her as she would hiss and snarl, approaching me and backing off several times, before eating the food only a couple feet away. I suppressed my fear of being torn to shreds. Then I guess she decided that I was not a threat and she flipped over on her back and let me reach out to scratch her chin. Thus began our friendship.

Among Cleo's three kittens, unfortunately, there was one male and he did not survive for long because the wild male cats in the area would kill off all male offspring. So I was left with two females, who in amazingly short time grew into adults and began to produce their own kittens. It wasn't long before I had five adult female cats that I was feeding. They were, however, only outside cats so it didn't really matter how many lived in my bajo.

Edna and Walter finally were able to move into their house next door and we began a friendship that lasts to this day. Edna was a wonderful cook and I swear she could turn dish water into something delectable. Periodically they would throw dinner parties and for several days before hand Edna could be found in her kitchen with her head tied up in a bandana. It was so very hot anyway there in Limon and when she got started on one of her cooking binges the kitchen would heat up to almost unbearable temperatures. She decided to campaign for an air conditioner to be put into the window, but, knowing her husband as she did, she had to "go in the back door" to get one. So she hung a large thermometer where he would be sure to see it and it wasn't too long before he came up with the idea of putting an air conditioner in there. I have learned a lot from this woman!

One famous dinner party, forever dubbed "The Giant Omelet," was given to honor some friends of theirs who were visiting. Edna began early and Mary and I were going to be her helpers, you know, chopping veggies and stuff. Things were going smoothly; Edna would bark orders and we would hop to it. So she said to us, "Please separate those eggs in the refrigerator." I swear, that is what we both heard. We dutifully opened the frig to see 6–7 dozen eggs stacked in there and we began to place the yolks in one bowl and the whites in another. Now, we were not more than a few feet away from Edna during this process, so it did not occur to us that she was too busy to see what we were doing. Finally we finished all seven dozen eggs and reported our feat to the chef. She looked at us and then at our carefully separated eggs and said, "What Have You Done?" We replied with the obvious answer and she said, "No, I wanted you to separate the old eggs from the new eggs," which were sitting out on the counter nearby. Those separated eggs became a giant omelet for guests the next morning and another story went into the hopper.

Edna also taught me a variation on the card game of canasta called "foot." We played most every day and kept track of winnings and losings. The prize to the winner would be lunch and a movie in San Jose the next time we went there. And when we played, it was for <u>blood</u>. There was no mercy shown whatsoever. We laid out all our aggressions on that card table. I think now that we saved ourselves thousands of dollars on shrinks.

When it was time for our trip to San Jose, we would take the train because Edna did not like to fly. We would book "first class" and this was the caboose car which had some tables with wooden benches facing them. This was very convenient because we could play "foot" along the 6 hour ride, never missing an opportunity to draw blood. The ride would begin early in the morning and the first part ran along the ocean to the north before it cut inland heading west. We would travel through the coconut plantations where the coconuts were harvested for oil, the main staple of the local diet. Then we would begin to get into the hills and on into the mountains, all the while following this beautiful rapidly flowing river. At times we would peer out

Limon, Costa Rica

the window and down the edge of the mountain to tremendous depths. The train would be rocking back and forth and you would say a little prayer that it would stay on the tracks to get you through this dangerous area. And there was one long bridge we had to cross. The train would slow to a snail's pace and inch its way across. I always had to close my eyes.

The vendors were not allowed in our car. We were "first class," you know. But they would be by the track outside at every stop along the way. I don't believe I ever bought anything besides peanuts which I could shell myself because all the things to eat seemed so very handled. Who knew how long it had been out in the open among the heat and flies.

When we arrived at the station in San Jose there was this big rush of people all vying for the same taxi. But eventually it got sorted out and we would find our way to the company apartment where we would spend the night. Shopping was only a short walk away and the whole next day we would make several trips out and return to drop off our goodies. Here in San Jose they had real supermarkets, hair salons, shoe stores and fabric stores. Plenty of ways to spend your pesos. Another night at the apartment and then we would make the journey home on the train. The shopping from that trip would have to last us for 6 months. Twenty years later when I returned to San Jose for a visit, the hotel advertised its touring events, and one was "THE JUNGLE TOUR" which was that same train ride to Limon. Who would have believed it would turn into this? I felt like a real pioneer.

My bug collecting continued and my reputation as The Bug Lady increased. There was one friend from Trinidad who had a young son about two years old who was just beginning to talk. He was always a bit confused with English and Spanish as his mother would use only English and the maids, who took care of him, spoke only Spanish. They were trying to teach him the word for butterfly which was "mariposa," but that was a very long word. So one day my friend called up to ask me please to hurry down to her house because she had a large beetle on her veranda. Away I went and ran quickly up her steps. When little Stuart saw me he began to scream, "PUTA, PUTA!!" To him all critters were butterflies, but he could not pronounce mariposa, so it came out "puta" which means whore in Spanish. I survived the character slam, but Stuart, I am quite sure, has never lived that story down.

    There was bug collecting of another kind which was not nearly as fun. They were called amoeba and were a constant threat there in the tropics. You just never knew who would be handling your food in a restaurant, so you tried to order only cooked items, never salads or raw things. And, of course, there was the water too that may be contaminated. So in time you began to recognize the symptoms of having amoeba and would visit your doctor.

There was this one time when things were different, however. The symptoms of constant stomach ache, nausea when eating anything, aching all over and being tremendously tired, not to mention the diarrhea, all began to weigh me down. It just went on and on and I couldn't seem to get back on my feet with any medication I tried. Finally I went to a doctor and when he examined my stool, he found that I had <u>nematodes.</u> Now my husband was a nematologist by profession and when these microscopic worms invade a banana plant, you inject it with Nemagon using a gigantic 5 gallon syringe. So right away he suggested that he give me a shot, which I declined. These critters were a bit different than the usual, and the remedy was to take a very strong narcotic. Before doing that, however, I was supposed to first get rid of most of my symptoms with a

Limon, Costa Rica

different medication, but that medication was not working at all. So I just decided, enough is enough, and I took the narcotic which was about a tablespoon of the stuff mixed into coca cola, taken one dose each morning for three days. Well, I soon found out what it is like to be HIGH. I was walking around the house a foot off the floor, running into doors and not caring at all. But it did the job and, after having been sick for two months, I began to heal. The hitch to this remedy was that I became addicted to coca cola (even without the narcotic) for many months until I could finally wean myself away from it. Another lesson (although tiny in comparison) to appreciate what addicts go through to kick a habit.

Our company had several small planes in order to fly the men around to various plantations in the area, and periodically these planes would need to fly to Panama City for a checkup. The manager's wife and I decided that it would be fun to ride along for the 48 hour round trip. But it would not be much of a story if it were that simple. The day we were supposed to drive out to the airport, which was down a dusty gravel road to this cement strip laid right next to the sandy beach on the ocean, the inhabitants of Limon decided to stage a strike. I forget their grievance, but their plan was to close off that road to the airport since it was the vital link to the city. Most of the supplies to the city were flown in on cargo planes, so it was a good plan. But not so great for June and myself. We were determined, however, to not let anyone rain on our parade, so we decided to hire two boys to carry our suitcases and we would walk the two miles down that dusty road.

It took a while and our sweat had turned to mud from the dust, but we climbed aboard that company plane and flew away. It was only about a one hour flight to Panama City and a nice shower at our hotel was very welcome. But we had only 24

1971–1973

hours now to do our shopping, so no time to waste. There were lovely things to buy there and I found a lace tablecloth and some molas, the local Indian appliqué pieces. We had a wonderful time, and that evening I discovered that there was a casino in the hotel. June had never gambled before, so we decided that we would take $2 and play a machine. That lasted about two minutes, so June said she understood that I meant $2 EACH. Already I could see that she was hooked and I felt somewhat responsible for leading her down that slippery path.

The next morning we had to get up early for our flight home. We didn't know what would be waiting for us at the airport in Limon, but it wasn't long before we learned that the strike was still on and we were going to have a problem to get home. The manager's wife was in the plane, however, so I wasn't worried. Somehow they would take care of us. Because we had been to a neighboring country, we had to clear customs just like at any airport. So a pickup truck had been sent out to meet the plane with the man from customs. He was a huge man and they had put him in a lawn chair in the back of a pickup. We soon appreciated his dedication to his job when we learned how this pickup truck had gotten to the airport, because we had to take the same route to get back into the city. It was a ride way out around the city, down dirt roads pitted with potholes and I could only think about that big man sitting in his chair in the back of that truck being jostled as we were, but having to hang on to that rickety chair in the process.

We did not get too many visitors while we lived in Costa Rica so it was always a pleasure when family came. Johannes' parents and one sister from Holland made the trip, and it was his mother's first plane ride. And what a trip it was. At one point between Florida and San Jose, the plane hit an air pocket and dropped. I don't care who you are, that is an event to make your heart land in your stomach. Toward the end of their visit, she told Johannes that she was worried about the return trip and having to go through that air pocket again.

Neither of his parents spoke English, so it was a challenge for me to entertain them while Johannes was at work. But his sister spoke a little English and would translate for me as she could. I began to notice that Moeker (mother in Dutch), would take a long time in the bathroom in the morning. Well, you know, some people are slow, so I was not too concerned, but I learned later the real reason. You see, Moeker's whole life was mostly dedicated to cleaning house when she wasn't raising their seven children. Now, she was not allowed to do this (or so she thought) because she was at her daughter-in-law's house. So she would go into the bathroom, close the door, and clean the room from top to bottom – EVERY MORNING. That was one clean bathroom, and hey, whatever floats your boat is what I say. Vader's thing was to take long walks with a walking stick that he had fashioned from a branch. He would be gone for a couple hours sometimes and the thing is that he never shed his long underwear the whole time, even with our 90 degree/90% humidity. That's a good Dutch farmer for you. My husband has those same genes and loves to suffer. I never argue because you can't easily fight heredity.

My neighbor, Edna, was always eager to grow lovely plants and had heard that the butts of old cigars crumbled up and placed in the soil around a plant would do wonders. So with that in mind she would come over to collect the old cigars which Vader had finished to put them to good use. Moeker noticed this curious business and, not understanding the English that gave the reason for it, she assumed that we had very poor neighbors and suggested to Johannes that he buy some new cigars for Walter so he wouldn't have to smoke the butts from Vader.

Moeker would always help me peel the potatoes and clean up after meals. My main concern during their visit was what to feed them, what with our limited grocery shopping in town. Somehow I managed. But an indication of our problem with the language barrier came one meal when I wanted to serve ice cream for dessert. I asked around the table for those who wanted some, and my sister-in-law said, "Yes, I will have a piece of ice." OK, I thought, the lady wants to chew on an ice cube, it's very hot here, so I will try to please her. I brought out a small bowl of ice cubes and placed it in front of her. There was this look on her face like – What in the hell is this? I learned that you can't sometimes translate literally from one language to another. A "piece of ice" meant a little bit of ice cream. After an embarrassed laugh, she got her ice cream. We remain friends.

My own sister, her husband and 5 year old daughter, Jill, came to visit us too during our stay in Limon. No language obstacles there. We had a great time going to Playa Bonita which was just north of town. It was one of those places that could have been in a magazine that advertises tropical beaches. There was a wide expense of white sand in this small cove with lots of palm trees. The waves were mesmerizing but there was a strong undertow so it was not a good place to swim.

At the end of their visit we flew up to San Jose to tour around the central valley. There are so many lovely places to visit, one being the gold museum where there is, I think, the world's largest collection of Pre-Colombian gold artifacts. There is a vault deep in the structure where they turn off the lights and close the doors behind you as you enter. When they turn the lights on again, the shine of the gold is almost blinding. It will make a big impression on you, and certainly impressed my 5 year old niece. On the way out you can't help but visit the museum store and that is where my niece bought me a gift of some gold reproduction Pre-Colombian frog earrings. I have worn these earrings almost exclusively for 35 years. Here is another fast forward. When we at last retired and moved to Las Vegas, I lost one of those earrings. I was devastated, but as luck would have it, this same niece had finished her degree in art and was an excellent jewelry maker. I sent her the remaining earring and she made a reproduction of my reproduction. So I am wearing them again and I have told the story behind my earrings to many, many people. How great is that?

There was a company school in town which was not only for company kids but for the general populace also. It was called the Lincoln International School and most of the classes were taught in English. The kids who entered primary school were not as yet speaking English, so it was imperative that they begin in first grade to learn the language. During that first year of my living in Limon, about ten weeks before the semester was over, there was some big turmoil in the school and several of the teachers left, which made a big hole they needed to fill. It came to their attention that Mrs. Klink "was a teacher" (remember my correspondence classes I taught in Pandora), and would I be willing to fill in? I resisted and resisted, but they kept increasing the amount they would pay me until finally my husband began to twist my arm too. So I gave in and began to teach phonetics to the first grade class. Not so bad, you may be thinking. But what you don't know is that none of these kids spoke English, I was not allowed to speak Spanish, and I had them right after recess. They were NEVER ready to sit down and learn phonetics and I had no idea of how to make them do that. It was a constant test of wills and I doubt seriously that they learned a thing under my tutelage. I endured for those 10 weeks until the end of the semester and then made sure that nobody EVER AGAIN would ask me to teach kids. Wave as much money in front of my face as you want, it just was not going to happen, punto.

A cheap way to get back to the States was to hitch a ride on a banana boat. These were ships that transported the green bananas from Costa Rica to Gulfport, Mississippi, and they would carry 4–5 passengers at times too. I needed a shopping trip to the States so decided to make the trip. My roommate was a woman and her dog who were moving back to the States and she did not want to travel by plane with her dog. I was cool with sharing the room with the dog because he was a very gentle medium sized mutt, very friendly. The woman, I have forgotten her name, treated that dog like a child and would talk baby talk to him, which I thought a bit strange. We were facing a three day journey, and the problem began that first evening when "Jane" took the dog out for his evening walk, which, of course, was along the deck of the ship on which there was not a single blade of grass. Now she had trained her dog well to only do his business on grass, so there was the problem – no grass, no pee. She got down on her knees and pleaded with him but it was useless. And this went on for <u>two days</u>! The dog was obviously in great distress, and that night, somewhere in the middle of the night, he exploded – all over our room. But there was no reprimand from Jane. She gave him a big hug and told him what a good dog he was. I thought it was so funny I almost cried too.

You learn things in many ways in your life, sometimes through study, sometimes through observing, and sometimes the hard way. This was a lesson that definitely came the hard way. I had always thought of myself, up to that point, as cool and calm under pressure. I may fall apart afterwards, but I could be counted on to act with intelligence under pressure. Not so, said the Universe, and just so you understand, we are going to throw you a curve.

That day I had taken the train back to Pandora to visit some friends while Johannes was away for several days on business. As could be predicted, the return train was very delayed, waiting for other banana trains to pass first, and we sat for hours in the pitch black of the forest. I didn't get back to Limon until around 11pm and I caught a taxi to bring me to my house. As I paid off the cab and started walking up the driveway, I saw that the back door of the house was open!!

Oh My God! My only thought was to run into the house – not a good idea I know, but there is that "action under pressure" thing I had yet to learn about myself. My first observance was that the lock on the back door had been torn apart. What was missing? I raced around the house trying to assess the things missing, a radio here and small appliance there. Then on into the bedroom and I found our closet ripped apart with things strewn all over the floor. My jewelry box had been ransacked.

Then I stopped because a thought suddenly passed through my mind that the robber MIGHT STILL BE IN THE HOUSE. What to do? I better call down to the people who lived next to the guard house at the base of the hill and have them send the guard up to stay the night in my bajo. So I dialed the number, but when someone came on the line, I was totally unable to speak my name. Try as I might, nothing came out. They kept saying, "Who is this?" Finally I squeaked out my name and need. They came storming up the hill, waving a gun and they wanted to fire off a few rounds, but I didn't think that a good idea. They called yet another neighbor who came up with their dog which they offered to have stay with me too. After looking around in the house, checking all the closets and all, it was declared that the robber was gone. They all thought it best to call the police in the morning and everyone went home when

I assured them that I would be OK. But once alone in the house, I again went into panic mode remembering that my back door was completely wide open and, although the robber might not be in the house, he could well be in the bushes outside waiting to return. After all, there were still plenty of things to steal. So I called the Zellers again and this time they found the guard who came up and spent the night in my bajo.

I learned that day that you can never be too sure of how you will act in any given situation. You can hope that you will be calm and act intelligently, but that might not be the case. I have since given others a lot of rope when they have their challenges, because I have been there.

It was Christmas of 1972 and our by now good friends Edna and Walter were planning to go to Managua, Nicaragua, to spend the holiday with Edna's sister and her husband. They lived on the upper floor of a downtown hotel and he was working for the company in that country. Edna had gone on ahead of Walter and he was to follow on Christmas Eve. That night there was a huge earthquake in Nicaragua, at least 7 points on the seismic scale, and Walter was unable to leave Costa Rica. We all gathered down at the manager's house where there was a ham radio. He was able to contact another ham radio operator there in Managua who was reporting on the scene, and this man was saying that all of the city was on fire and there were dead bodies laying everywhere along the streets. The city was in ruins. It turns out that 10,000 people died that night. We all sat in stunned silence around that room in Limon, each coping in our own way, and collectively we were praying for the safety of Edna, her sister Louise and husband Bill. There was absolutely no way for us to find out if they were alive or dead.

At one point I decided to go into a bedroom to be by myself and said a prayer for my friend. Then, as if a physical

Limon, Costa Rica

wave of water had washed over me, there came a sense of absolutely knowing that she was OK. I just knew it and I returned to the living room and began to assure the group that Edna was alive and well.

Later that Christmas morning the company provided a plane for Walter to fly to the farm outside Managua and from there possibly he could make his way into the city to find Edna. While he was still in the air, word came to us that the manager of the Nicaraguan division had filled his jeep with water and other provisions and with a couple others had made his way into the city, heading for the company office in the center of the town. In the meantime, my friend Edna, Louise and Bill and their dog had been able to get out of the hotel, even though the first three floors had collapsed leaving the fourth floor hanging but in tact. In the process some timbers had fallen and hit Louise in the head. They started walking through the streets heading for the company office which was a low building and perhaps had survived. It was pitch black but the fires around them lit the way. When they got to the office, it indeed was still standing and they were able to enter. They stayed there until many hours later the manager from the farm found them and they all piled into his jeep for the journey out of town to the farm. The dog died along the way. When Walter arrived from Costa Rica, he found them all safe, and aside from Louise's wounds from which she never fully recovered and the dog that died, all was well.

We got news that Walter and Edna would be coming back to Limon and would arrive the next day. I decided to make a big welcome for them, and since I had the key to their house, I went over there and put streamers all over the place and cut out a big sign that said Welcome Home. At last they drove up and I ran out to greet Edna with a big hug. She was all wrapped up in a trench coat and I kept trying to remove it because of the heat, but she would not let me do that – for good reason. She had only her underwear on beneath that coat. She had given all her clothes to her sister who had lost everything in the earthquake. When she opened the door to her house, she burst into tears, which was the first time she had allowed herself to cry in the whole ordeal. Now there's a strong woman!

I wanted to end my stories from Limon on an upbeat, so I have chosen to tell you about The Halloween Party. This was the same year of 1972 but before the earthquake in Managua. The invitations went out about one month before and the party was to be held at one of the larger homes on the hill. They began decorating weeks before hand, hanging ghosts, goblins, witches and ghouls from the trees in their large yard and on the inside they had built a faux fireplace in order to have a mantle. The mantle would hold the first prize to be given for best costume, and it was in a box shaped like a small coffin, inside of which was a bottle of Bloody Mary. (As an aside to this story, the couple who won that first prize had come to Limon from Pandora. On their return trip on the train the next day, they placed that small coffin in their lap and pretended to cry all the way home. So they have a good story to tell too.)

We all spent hours coming up with costumes to wear and I decided that Johannes and I would be a caterpillar and the butterfly. I had a swimming suit of a brown fuzzy material and added some wings made of a sheer, rainbow colored, shiny material. Johannes's outfit would be made of a green fabric and the pants had feet hanging off the sides of them. The shirt also had feet and a pocket on the front in which I put a piece of the wing fabric from my butterfly outfit. He wore a headdress with antennae and pompoms on the ends.

Limon, Costa Rica

That night as we entered the house, we were greeted by the host who was dressed as Count Dracula. He put one hand on my back and I let out a scream because it wasn't really his hand but a rubber glove filled with ice. When Johannes entered in his caterpillar costume, they immediately decided that he was a nematode (never mind that nematodes don't have legs), so all my clever hints of a connection between his costume and mine went down the tubes. The beer began to flow and the party got louder and louder. Lots of laughing and dancing, especially by my husband. He sometimes would go a little crazy when he danced and you sort of had to just let him do his own thing. That evening he was jumping up and down, and everyone decided that he must be doing "the nematode stomp" and it became the dance rage.

The reason I called this The Halloween Party is that it went down in company history as one of the best parties ever. It was talked about for years. It certainly came back to haunt Johannes a short time later when we were transferred to Davao City in the Philippines. In January of 1973 we were sent on a "look see" trip to Davao in order to find a house and see what we needed to bring along, and when Johannes went into what would be his new office, there on the desk was a folder which, when he opened it, had a photograph of him in his "nematode" suit. It said, "This is who you will be getting."

On the last day of our packing for this transfer, with the last large wooden crate being sealed in my bajo, two of my five female cats decided to give birth at the same time down in my laundry room. First one had five kittens and she was "helped" by the other female who would press up against her in the corner. When number one had finished, the second one began her labor and produced four. So there I was with the original five adult female cats and now nine babies. The new people moving into the house already knew about the adults, but not the babies.

I was running around doing all those final things you do during a move and still trying to check in on the progress of the mothers. My neighbor's maid popped her head in, saw what was happening, and asked me if she could possibly have the two mothers with their kittens. She lived in a very poor section of town with many mice, and cats were welcome. I could have kissed her. I now could leave with a sense of relief that all my babies would be OK.

DAVAO CITY, THE PHILIPPINES
1973–1977

Davao City, the Philippines

When we were told of our transfer to the Philippines, I was extremely excited to be going to live in Asia. My dreams of world travel were all coming true and I could hardly wait to begin this new chapter of my life. But it was an exhausting journey of at least three days to get there from Central America. We first flew up to San Francisco where the head office of the company was located. We spent the night there and Johannes had some meetings before we continued on our way. From there the flight was about 15 hours to Manila. There were several routes the plane might take, one through Guam, another through Tokyo, and I don't remember just how we went, but I do remember being tired and greatly in need of a bath when we finally arrived in Manila. Another night was spent there before taking our last flight to Davao City which was located about 500 miles south on the big island of Mindanao.

The company put us up at a hotel right on the Bay of Mindanao and we spent the next four months there waiting for our shipment of household goods to arrive from Costa Rica. We had the dining hall menu memorized by then, and many times when I would call down for room service, all I had to do was give my room number and they knew what the order would be. We would eat most of our meals out on the patio of our room overlooking the swimming pool and gardens, with the water of the bay beyond. At times while we were sitting there, one of the gardeners would climb up to the top of a coconut tree to collect a liquid that the trees would secrete into a bamboo bucket, and this would be fermented into a local brew called "tuba." On occasion, one of these buckets would fall to the ground and you could smell it clear up to the second floor where we were sitting. How could anyone drink something that smelled so bad?

During those months, I went hunting for a house and finally found a split level, almost new home in a small subdivision, not too far from the office. Since I had sold all my furniture before leaving Costa Rica, I also was busy ordering new rattan furniture to be made for us. All you needed was a photograph of what you wanted and they could make it.

Just before I moved in I hired my live-in maids, yes maids with an "s." I had been told that you had to have at least two girls because they got too lonely by themselves. And since their salaries were only $10 a month (plus food, of course), it seemed like a good idea. I really got lucky and came upon two very good girls, highly recommended as being hard workers and good cooks. They seemed delighted to work for me too because we had no children and their work would be easier. I turned the whole lower level of the house over to them as there was a large living room plus their bedroom and bath.

This was my first experience with a live-in maid and in the beginning I had to resist doing things around the house because they already had so few chores with only the two of us to clean after. So every day the house was cleaned top to bottom, floors mopped, laundry done and kitchen spotless. I got used to it real fast and Johannes loved it since, being Dutch, he expected his home to be super clean. That's what Dutch women do, you know. The fact that he had married an American had not registered with him, apparently, so having maids to do all my housework worked out well for everyone.

To complete my family I wanted to get a cat. Johannes had told me flat out, <u>No More Cats</u> (I guess he was thinking of the 14 cats I had left in Costa Rica), but I replied that it was either a cat or a baby – take your pick. So a cat it was. An American neighbor had just had a litter of Siamese kittens and I went to choose one but came home with two, Sweet William ("Willy") and Sweet Charity ("Cheri"). They were six weeks old but as soon as I got them home I could see something was not right. They began to have attacks where they would leap into the air, scream in pain and fall down unable to walk. I would scoop them up, race down to a local vet, who was a large animal vet but the only one in town, and he would inject them with something and they would be good for a while. Then it would happen again, each time they lost a little ground and it got so bad that I did not expect them to live. Finally the vet said he would try some calcium, and that was the answer. These kittens had rickets and as soon as they started getting those calcium shots their health improved rapidly and soon they were running up and down the stairs.

Cheri proved her worth one day while I was upstairs sleeping and Johannes was in the living room reading the paper. Suddenly he saw the cat take off after something in the middle of the red shag rug. It was a snake – a deadly bamboo viper snake to boot, so thin that it probably came in under the front door. Johannes ran out to the kitchen yelling for the maids and these two tiny girls who came up to about his waist grabbed the "snake stick" and ran into the living room to kill the thing, thus rescuing my husband. Those girls may have been small but they were fearless.

One of our first major purchases was a car for me. It was a Japanese banana yellow Minica, a two cylinder, hatch back, two door car that mixed oil and gas like a motor bicycle. It cost $2000 and was so small that I easily learned how to change the spark plugs and oil. If the battery was low, my girls could simply give me a little push and I would be on my way. There was one major drawback to driving this car and that was that it was also the local taxi for Davao and there were a thousand of them around town. So everywhere I went I would be hailed by someone needing a ride and I had to be careful to lock the doors when parking because you just might find someone sitting in your car when you returned.

The issue of language was quite interesting in Davao. Tagalog was proclaimed the official language of the Philippines and this was probably because the president of the country came from a district in the north speaking that language. This meant that schools had to teach in Tagalog which would be a second language to most Filipinos. There in Davao the local language was Cebuano. I was feeling an urge to learn "Filipino," but I soon learned that it was a dilemma just which one to learn, Cebuano (which would allow me to speak to the locals) or Tagalog which most of the locals could speak but not fluently. I zeroed in on the latter and decided to sign up for classes at a university downtown. Since I was not interested in receiving credit, I would audit the class. There was no such thing as a computerized system to sign up for a class, so you had to make your way through this maze of tables, at each of which I explained my special status and was assured I was on the right path. However, when I reached the end, I could see that I was signed up as a regular student. Oh well, that would have to be the way it was. So my next question was, "What day do classes begin." I got several answers from various official looking people, and basically my guess was as good as theirs. So I showed up on campus on a Monday which seemed to be a good day to begin classes. With a room number in hand, I began to try to find the room, climbing to the top floor of this building and then that building. At last I actually found the room, only to find a note on the door that the room had been changed because the teacher could not climb so many stairs. Half my day had been spent, at this point, just to find the class. I was the only foreigner in the whole class, but sticking out like a sore thumb had long ago ceased to faze me. Then it happened, the teacher began to talk – IN THE LOCAL CEBUANO DIALECT. Now, all along my path of registration I had repeatedly asked the question, "Will this class be taught in English," and was assured <u>repeatedly</u> that it would. So I immediately raised my hand to point this out to the teacher. She looked at me and said, "Well, I cannot take the time to repeat everything in English to you. You should find yourself a tutor." I stood up, walked out, and that was my last attempt to learn Filipino.

Early on in living in Davao I discovered Hula and I was amazed at how large a role it would play in my life. It began as a fun way to get exercise that several of the company ladies were doing and they invited me to join them. I had to really persevere in the beginning because I was placed in the beginner's class which was entirely children who came up to my knee. They all seemed to take to the idea of doing one thing with your hands and another with your feet – sort of like rubbing your stomach with one hand and patting your head with the other. I could get one thing going pretty well but when I tried to add the other, I became this spastic person. Would I EVER get this? It came to me suddenly, however, and I soon advanced to the adult class.

Periodically there would be a recital and we would perform for one organization or another. It was a tremendous challenge for me because I would be so nervous that my knees would shake. That's not pretty so I had a little secret that I will reveal here that helped me get out there on that stage – it was called gin. I learned that I could have one drink and still remember the dance and be relaxed enough to do my dance without shaking. This secret came back to bite me, however, a couple years later when I was going to be performing at a luau out at our company pineapple plantation. The party was around the pool and the liquor was flowing. I kept waiting and waiting for the program to begin, but the organizers were having way too much fun to get things going. I had my one gin with tonic, but after a while I felt the "edge" sliding away from me, so I had another. And then another. Well, by that time I pretty much didn't care when the program would begin. I was loose! I think I did dance, and in my eyes I did a wonderful job, but I can't truthfully know that for sure.

During those years when I would return to Florida to visit my parents, Mom would always throw a big luau party around the pool and I would be the entertainment. I would have to dance for around 45 minutes and one time I even got my picture in the local paper. That was my 15 seconds of fame, I guess.

Davao City had a large community of international families, some there representing their countries with the diplomatic corps, some with various companies, like our company of Dole out of Hawaii (at that time). With all our men away at work all day, we ladies formed groups for social activities. One was a sewing club which was much more about talking and eating than sewing. But we all would bring something to work on. For me it usually was a piece of cross stitch or embroidery, and since it was difficult to talk and sew without making mistakes, my project would mostly lay in my lap.

Then there was the mah jong group to which I very soon became addicted. This is the Chinese tile game which has many forms, depending on what country you live in. Our form was a mixture of Chinese and Filipino, and it resembled gin rummy in some ways. Every week we would have a table or two and played for pennies. We would meet around 9am and play the entire day until we had to race out to beat our husbands home.

And then there was the women's auxiliary at a local hospital. Anyone new coming to town was generally roped in and put to work. We ran a small gift shop at the hospital and someone had to be in charge of the buying of supplies down in Chinatown. That fell to me after a while and I became acquainted with the little shops selling all manner of trinkets. I learned to beg for our cause too, which was great practice in the art of haggling in the Third World. Later I became treasurer of the group and had the "pleasure" of doing all the banking. I would spend hours waiting in several lines to accomplish what should have been the simple feat of making a deposit in a matter of minutes. In the final two years of our stay in Davao, I presided as the president of the woman's auxiliary, and this meant that I had the privilege of doing most of the work.

Each year we would have a rummage sale and would spend months gathering stuff from the backs of closets and donations from companies. Then we would lay it all out in a gym sized room up at the hospital. With all our floor people in place, we would open the doors to this huge rush of local people, and the madhouse would begin. It was truly a feat to emerge at the end of the day with your shoes still on your feet. But the resulting money that we earned would pay for medications for those who couldn't afford it, or we would buy a new piece of equipment for the maternity ward. Each year we would find one deserving family and buy all the kids' school clothes and other items that they needed. The experience was worth the effort.

Along with these social activities, there were also the times when we would actually include our men folk in our plans, like when we would plan a trip to Picnic Island on a Sunday. We would hire a boat that could hold a group of people and head out toward an unoccupied island near the mouth of the bay. Once we landed we would have to carry all our picnic paraphernalia to the other side where there was this wide expanse of white sandy beach. The coral reef surrounding this beach made it impossible to land a boat over there. But we always had about 10–15 people so with everyone carrying something, we easily were able to set up our picnic. The whole day would be spent on, in or near the water. Snorkeling was great because of the reef and there was one memorable time when I was out there bobbing around in the waves that I came across a lion fish. They are so beautiful with all their "veils" but are also poisonous. I had to back up and away and find a different avenue through the reef.

When the tide was out you could find great shells and interesting driftwood pieces. Some people, however, would choose to just find a palm tree and sack out underneath. By late afternoon we knew we had to pack up, trudge back across the island and make the one hour ride home. The water would always be very choppy by then, and we were tired, sticky with salt and gritty with sand, but it was a day well spent.

About one year after I had arrived in Davao, our good company friends. Edna and Walter, joined our Filipino division and moved into a company house in the adjoining subdivision. Edna was so excited to get the chance to live in Asia, just as I was, and we picked up our foot card game right where it left off. We also introduced the entire group of women to the game and began to have "foot days."

It wasn't long before Walter, Edna and I began a quest to discover the best shelling beach on Mindanao. We would head out on a Sunday morning to some obscure beach that we had heard about and spend the day collecting bags and bags of shells. One such beach was south of town at least an hour's drive away. We finally came to a small town perched on the edge of the bay, but the sand was a black color and had not a single shell. By this time it was noon and we were ready to eat

Davao City, the Philippines

our picnic lunch, so we started driving back toward Davao to a spot we had seen where the road ran right along the beach. We found a place to park the car and opened the trunk to get our picnic gear out, but as soon as we set foot on that beach we began to find shells strewn everywhere. It was "shell heaven" so, with sandwich in hand, we began to fill our bags with treasurers. Our bags soon became too much to carry, so we hired a couple little boys to follow along and be our pack horses.

Another beach we had heard about was the "disappearing island" out in the bay, said to have good shelling. The island would appear when the tide was down, and a person was notified ahead to go "bait" the island with the entrails of chickens to attract shells. The next day we timed our embarkation just before the tide went out so that when we arrived, there would be an island. There was, of course, only sand on that island, being in the middle of the bay, so the heat was intense. And to top it off, we didn't find a single shell. We headed back to the pier, but because the tide was out, we could not get close and had to wade knee deep in squishy, thick mud to reach the pier. This lesson was, I guess, you can't believe everything people tell you.

And what did we do with all those shells? Well, since we were all very creative people, we used a large share of them to frame mirrors and put under glass on top of tables and even trade them with other people who were also "shellers." I always kept a basket full of my junk stuff, and when I had a visitor come to my home with children, the kids were allowed to dig through the basket and take home whatever treasurers they found.

I kept my main collection of shells, my "gee whiz collection," displayed on a metal and glass shelf that I had built for me down at a local metal shop. I went in there with a drawing of this five shelf unit with a sort of bamboo design on the metal supports, and they were able to do a pretty good job of copying it. If you come to my home today, you will still find that same shelf with shells. The only difference is that I am the one who has to dust it today.

When you live in the "boondocks" of the world, you have to learn to be very creative and self sufficient. In those days there were no large department stores or Home Depots or even big supermarkets. So you learned to make do or try substitutes or have something made. As with my metal display shelves, you would just find a picture in a magazine and take it to the local furniture maker. So this is where I went with my design for a floor loom. Ever since taking a class in weaving at the University of Wisconsin many years previous, I had dreamed of having a floor loom. This furniture maker had never seen a loom before and the problem I had with him is that he was somewhat of a male chauvinist and would not accept that I knew what I was talking about with my design. He had his own ideas, in spite of the fact that he had no idea of how a loom functioned. He kept wanting to change this and wanting to change that. Finally I gave up and went to someone else who was very willing to build what I had drawn. The result was a four harness jack loom which was somewhat of a clunker, but it worked.

My next challenge was to find materials to weave in this city with its primitive selection of cords and yarns. I did the best I could, however, and with the help of some books I had brought with me from the States, I taught myself pattern weaving. Weaving suited my personality perfectly because just when you were about to get tremendously bored with one phase of the task, you would finish and start the next part, from winding spools to threading to tying onto the front beam, tensioning the cords, and then the actual weaving. I found that the smaller the warp material used, the more challenging and therefore the more rewarding the adventure, and for many of my projects I used sewing thread for warp and weft. Can't get too much smaller than that.

Sandwiched between all my social events, I would find time to sew for myself too. One thing very available in Davao were fabric shops because most people had their clothing custom made. I also learned to sew shirts for my husband and for the next 20 years, all the shirts in his closet were hand made by me. There was once when I tried to sew a pair of pants for him too, but that failed miserably and I remember throwing them on the floor and stamping on them in pure frustration.

As I began to get interested in one craft or another, I would teach my girls (maids) each new thing I had learned. Every time I went back to the United States I would pick up several more books to learn some new craft, usually with an aim to learn something that did not require too much equipment. One such craft was macramé which was very popular at that time. It wasn't long before someone asked me if I would make a plant hanger for them and I realized that this could be a money making adventure. So I taught the girls the basics and began to take orders which began to pour in steadily. We had almost more than we could handle. It seemed that when one neighbor ordered something, the other had to have one too. Soon Fita had enough money to begin going to night school and Esther bought herself a sewing machine and took sewing lessons downtown.

At the same time as this little cottage industry business got going, I learned that it was really illegal for me to be doing this. I was "exploiting the local people" and, as a foreigner, I could not be involved in any way. So we kept it all word of mouth and thumbed our nose at the establishment. The girls were making some extra money and also filling in many hours around the house when they had nothing to do.

Since I was not making any money in this venture, I figured out a method of "payment" for me too. I wanted a quilted bedspread for our king size bed and asked the girls to do the quilting. First I built a quilting frame down in their living room and stretched the fabric and batting over that. They would sit every afternoon for a couple hours and hand quilted this whole pattern of all over green philodendron leaves on a cream background. I think I got the better end of the bargain since quilting, being so repetitious, is not something I enjoy.

To get away from the city, sometimes I flew in the small company plane out to the pineapple plantation of Kalsangi. It was located about a half hour flight away at the base of Mount Matutum, a dormant volcano. On the upper side of the plantation was the housing compound of about 40 homes built around a golf course. There was also the club house, large Olympic sized swimming pool and tennis courts. So the place was like a country club with cooler weather, being much higher than Davao. I always thought it would be lovely to live out there, but that was never to be.

One time a group of people from Kalsangi wanted to make a trip up to a mountain community where a native tribe was going to have a special festival. I joined them in a caravan of about five 4 wheel drive vehicles, the last of which carried a group of armed guards. We would be traveling through some dangerous territory, what with a war being waged between the Filipino government and a Muslim separatist group living on Mindanao. It was not unheard of that foreigners were abducted and held for ransom.

Soon after we started out, the way began to get very rough. The cars had to ford some rivers and claw their way up a

Davao City, the Philippines

road that was more a dry river bed. It took a couple hours to finally reach this Catholic mission up in the hills where the festival would take place, and the first thing I saw was a very large coca cola truck sitting there. Now, how the hell did that cumbersome truck get up there?

I knew that the tribe of people living in this area wore very special hats because I had seen one hanging on a friend's wall in Kalsangi. I approached the head priest to ask about buying a hat and he told me that I would probably not be able to do so because these hats held very special importance to the maker. However, very soon the word got out that this foreign lady wanted to buy a hat and a man approached me offering to sell me the chin strap from this hat. This was a very ornate beaded strap that had tassels on the end made of horse hair, and the strap would go under the chin with the tassels hanging down from where the strap attached to the hat. A gorgeous thing, but I indicated that I also wanted to buy the whole hat. The man motioned me to follow him to a family of tribal people sitting under a tree. What a beautiful group, all adorned with their intricately embroidered costumes. The woman took her hat off which had this specially appliquéd cloth draped over it. I paid whatever price they were asking because I had no bargaining power at that point. Stepping back out into the sun blazing down on us, I thought it would probably be 10 degrees cooler under that hat so I placed it on my head and was rewarded with instant coolness.

This is a long story, but stick with me. I was walking down the path a few moments later with another person and I must have said out loud, "Oh, my, I hope that woman didn't have lice!" After taking the hat off and feeling that sun again, I thought, oh well, and replaced it on my head. The rest of that day was spent watching horse fighting and other activities before our difficult trek down the hill.

Several months later I again went out to Kalsangi to visit my friend, who had not even been on the trip to the festival. The first thing she said when I came through her door was not "Hello, How are you?" No, it was, "I hear you had a bad case of head lice!" And she was expecting me to sleep in her guest room that night! You know the game played where someone begins whispering in the ear of the next person and they whisper to the next, and so on down a long line. Then you compare the story from beginning to end? I never had lice but somehow that story got told.

There was one memorable trip in the company plane out to the plantation. It would hold four people and that day I had to sit in the co-pilot's chair. This made me very uncomfortable as I really don't like to look at all those instruments. About half way through the journey, the pilot turned to me and said I should take over the controls, seeing as how I had one of those steering wheels in front of me also. I kept saying, "Please, no, I don't want to do this;" but he just took his own hands off his wheels and said I was in charge. I grabbed the wheel, afraid for our lives, and glued my eyes to that dial on the dash which indicates your wing position. A knot began to form in my belly, and that pilot is lucky I didn't pee in my pants! I do that, you know, in the face of gripping fear! At last he took control again for the landing, but it took me hours to get rid of that stomach ache. I guess _he_ thought it was funny but it was no joke to me.

The war between the separatist Muslim group and the Filipino government had a direct effect on all of us at that time because Ferdinand Marcos, the president, had placed martial law throughout the country. This meant that you could not be out on the street from midnight until dawn. All social events had

Davao City, the Philippines

to end about 11:30 to allow participants to return home before the curfew. There were a few times when Johannes and I broke that curfew and it was a scary thing to expect the police to be chasing you through the streets. We were lucky that this never happened to us, but we knew of others who were not so lucky.

I want to tell you about a fabulous trip that my friend Edna and I took. You see, we both had begun to collect baskets and had heard that there was this city north of Manila that was the Mecca of baskets. We had to go. It meant a flight up to Manila, an overnight there, and then another smaller plane up to the mountainous city of Baggio. We stayed at the Pines Hotel at the top of the hill in the city center and about five minutes after throwing our suitcases into our room, we were out the door of the hotel to walk down that hill to the open market. And it was truly "basket heaven" when we entered that crowded, bustling market. We could not contain ourselves and began buying baskets, one more beautiful than the next, large and small, new and antique. We had baskets within other baskets and were very soon at the limit of what we could carry, so we hired a taxi to take us back up to the hotel. But we could not stop there and headed down that hill again. This time we were a bit wiser and hired some small boys to help us carry our treasures. A second load was STILL not enough and down the hill we went again. About that time we took a breath and remembered that we had three days here and we probably should slow down. After having our lunch up at the restaurant there in the hotel we decided to visit some areas outside town that had various crafts they were selling. One place had wood carvings, another had silver that they were working into jewelry and yet another had hand woven articles. We were having the time of our lives and paid no particular attention as to how we could possibly transport all our goodies back to Davao.

1973–1977

It was at the weaving village that an incredible thing happened. (Cue in "It's a Small World" aka Disneyland.) Now I have to lay a little background on this story. While we were living in Costa Rica we had some friends who were from Brazil and they left the company to work at a university in the central valley. While they were there they had some neighbors who were from Holland and these people wanted to send a package back to their family through us since they heard that we were planning a trip to Holland soon. So they sent the package to us – we never met them in person. Now lets fast forward to our weaving village outside Baggio. I had entered the gift shop to look at the wares for sale and noticed a large piece hanging on the wall which I recognized to be from the south of the Philippines near where I lived. It had a fancy price on it, and there was a woman standing there admiring it. I heard her speaking Dutch with her friend so I struck up a conversation with her, saying that I was married to a man from Holland. Then I went on to talk about the woven piece. End of conversation.

Later that morning Edna and I went back to Baggio to eat our lunch up at the hotel and as we were sitting there, all of a sudden this same Dutch woman came striding up to our table and said to me, "Are you Mrs. Klink?" I was dumbfounded because, of course, I had not given her my name when we met at the gift shop. And here is the story. (Are you still humming "It's a Small World"?) She went back to where she was living there in Baggio and told her husband she had met an American, married to a Dutch man, living in Davao, and he immediately said, "Well, she must be the wife of Johannes Klink." He had heard that, like them, we had also moved to the Philippines from Costa Rica. She invited Edna and me to dinner at her home that evening, and I finally met the family for whom we had carried that package.

Davao City, the Philippines

On our last walk down that hill heading again to the market to see if there were possibly any baskets we missed, we passed by a shop piled high with antiques that just drew us into the door. Any woman would understand that feeling. As we walked through the main entry, a little old Chinese woman behind the counter looked up and exclaimed out loud, looking at Edna, "Oh, you are a woman with many friends!" This, of course, roped us right in and we spent the next hour having our fortunes told. And this was the first time that I had any idea of Edna's age which she never would tell me, because in order for the old woman to read her Chinese book of fortunes, she had to know exactly when you were born, the hour, day of week and date. So there it was, Edna's age, which I will not reveal here. Suffice to say that I was amazed.

When Edna and I made our journey back home, we had 17 pieces of luggage between us. The company sent a pickup out to the airport to meet us because there was no way we would fit into even two taxis. We were not ashamed at all, either, at our excessive spending. By the time I left Davao City, my collection of baskets numbered 150. One can never have too many baskets.

Some things could really happen anywhere. For instance, have you ever locked yourself out of your house? Murphy's Law usually applies, which meant, in my case, that Johannes was out of town, the maids had gone home for the weekend and it was hours before our evening guard would arrive, who didn't have a key anyway. And here I was without shoes. After checking all outside doors for any left unlocked and not even bothering with windows because they all had metal bars, I had to come up with a plan. I would try to make my way over to another home of a company wife in the next subdivision. But that meant walking down a gravel road for a distance, so I had to figure out how to manage in bare feet. Then I remembered that I had seen a pair of shoes that the maid had thrown into the garbage bin, so I fished them out. I think they were a size 2, or something, but at least my toes were covered, and I set off down the street. I was happy that I wasn't in my nightgown or something. My friend had a good laugh when she saw me in those size 2 shoes with my size 8 feet, but took me in to await the return of my husband the next day. One would think after this experience I would have hidden a key outside just for such emergencies, but I was not that wise yet.

I can't remember exactly the year, but during our stay we lived through a devastating earthquake that hit Mindanao. The epicenter was just off the coast of the southern tip of the island, but we felt it very strongly in Davao also. The resulting tsunami swept an entire village out to sea and there was an estimate of 10,000 people who lost their lives that night. Johannes was out at the pineapple plantation sleeping in the guest house which was built up on stilts. It rocked back and forth so violently that decorations on the walls came crashing down. In Davao, I was awakened by the bed moving across the room and the air conditioner cut out. I sat up on the edge of the bed as it started moving and thought I should probably get out of the house, but in those few seconds the movement subsided. I knew, however, that this was a "big one."

The news went out across the world of this huge earthquake, but it was reported as having been centered in Davao City. My parents in Florida heard the news and were worried about our safety, so they called the head office in San Francisco. They were told that, as far as was known, Davao had been spared. It was several days before the extent of damage could be assessed and we all learned of the huge devastation to the south of us.

Davao City, the Philippines

We had been living in the Philippines for almost five years, and I was on probably my last R and R trip to Kalsangi. That afternoon was spent at the home of a woman who a year earlier had moved there from the company's division in Thailand. She had gone on and on about how much she hated living in Thailand. The schools were so bad, the housing was terrible, this was lousy and that was awful. That evening we all gathered at a company party up at the club house and at some point Johannes called me aside to deliver some news – we were being transferred to Thailand. He was so excited, but couldn't understand my reaction of shock. We were to pack up the house and ship it off, but we would not leave ourselves until four months later.

This meant that we had to move into the guest house for the interim. It was situated next door to our dear friends Edna and Walter. Our two cats had a hard time adjusting to their new home, but really seemed to enjoy swinging on the lacy curtains. By the time we left, there were huge areas of shredded fabric, rendering the curtains a bit more "lacey" than when I came.

There was one advantage to living so close to Edna and that was due to the "batik mania" that overcame her and me after an artist friend had visited and taught Edna the basics of this craft. Batik is a very old Indonesian craft where hot liquid wax is painted onto cloth and forms a resist to subsequent dyes. We did not have very good quality dyes there in Davao, so we could not make clothing. The dyes would just leach out of the fabric if you would try to wash it. So we used an old iron and paper to blot out the wax in the finished pictures we were making. We didn't need to get all the wax out because it would only be a picture that you frame for the wall.

Early every morning I would peek through my ever more lacey curtains to see if the light was on in Edna's kitchen. This meant I could go over there, get the key to her basement studio where we worked, and begin to heat up the wax. With coffee in hand I would head over to get going on that day's masterpiece. There were times when we would literally forget to eat lunch because we would be so engrossed in our artistic adventures. What excitement we felt as we explored the wonderful things we could produce with this wax. And what a mess we made too with all that wax and paper. Our hands were stained with all colors of the rainbow, and it didn't even seem to matter, we were having such a lot of fun.

At last it came time for our move to begin and Murphy reared his head again. The very day of our scheduled flight to Manila, a typhoon hit. We waited to get the word if the plane would leave Davao or not. This presented a problem because I had planned to give my two cats a tranquillizer about 30 minutes before leaving the house, but I couldn't do this because when we got the word, we had to leave in that same moment, no chance to administer the pill. It was a one hour flight and the cats were put below with the luggage.

When we got to Manila, the plane landed safely, but due to the impending storm, there were no taxis or public transportation to get to our hotel. Usually a company car would pick you up, but today all we could do was sit with our luggage in an area that looked like a hangar, with jets screaming in our ears, the winds from the storm bearing down on us and little hope of surviving this ordeal. Finally a shuttle bus from our hotel – miracle of miracles – showed up and we were able to get away. The cats, poor babies, were so very traumatized that I feared for their sanity.

The next day the storm had passed and we had to get out to the airport again. This time I wanted to make sure that my babies were handled gently and asked an airline person to help

Davao City, the Philippines

me. She assured me over and over again that they would be treated with care and I should not worry. Then I saw through some big windows all the luggage going out to the airplane and there on top of the heap were my two cages which were TOSSED LIKE LUGGAGE up into the hold. I went screaming back to the desk, very upset at what I had just seen, but there was little that I could do at that point but say a prayer.

On that note we left the Philippines after living there for five years. I had very mixed feelings about not only leaving Davao, but going to Thailand, of which I had not heard too many good things. Each move, however, always seemed to bring new adventures, and I was getting accustomed to this Third World life. I realized much later, in looking back, that mine was anything but a normal life. This was brought into the spotlight for me when I sent my $5 away to my high school alumni group, along with a couple pages written about my life since leaving high school. They were making a special edition of their newspaper, and I figured they could edit my contribution to fit their space. To my great surprise, every word I had written was included, filling two columns on the page, even though all other contributions from classmates who had never left town and married the boy/girl next door were given only one inch space. Wow, that opened my eyes as to what a lucky girl I was!

HUA HIN, THAILAND

1977–1987

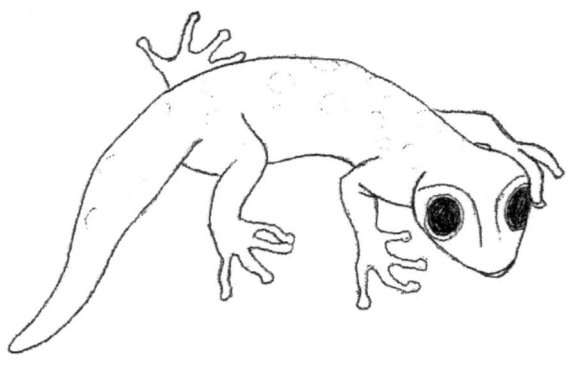

Hua Hin, Thailand

Our arrival in Thailand in 1977 was a continuation of the trauma of leaving Davao. As you remember, a typhoon had hit Manila as we were traveling through so it was in great exhaustion that we landed in Bangkok. My poor babies were not through with their ordeal yet. When I went to get them from the baggage claim, their cages came literally rolling down the ramp and I could do nothing but stand at the bottom and catch them. I was certain that if they didn't both have heart attacks, I would. We spent another night in Bangkok and in the morning made our two hour car ride south to the small fishing village of Hua Hin.

Hua Hin, meaning "head rock," is situated on the Bay of Siam about 100 miles south of Bangkok, and had, some 50 years previous, been a resort town. There were many homes built right on the beach which were now almost falling to the ground in disrepair. This was the state of the majority of housing in that small village so it was not easy for the company to find homes for the foreign personnel. We were about 10 families from various countries and our homes were scattered throughout the town. There was one main drag, which was the highway that ran from Bangkok south to the Malaysian border, and there were side streets, not all of them paved, that branched out from this road.

The home assigned to us was one of the old beach homes. The main house was on the second floor and there was a lanai and maid's quarters on the first floor. Above it had two small bedrooms, two baths, the kitchen and a living room/dining room central area. At the end of the living room toward the ocean there were floor to ceiling windows which were wonderful to enjoy the view, but the drawback was that, since we were only a few feet from the beach, we got all the salt spray. That makes a sticky mess and at least every week you had to clean those windows. We had a nice deck out front too which was a great place to enjoy your morning coffee and watch the fishing boats at the municipal pier just a short distance away.

We were not alone in that house, however. It took only one or two nights to realize that there was a huge colony of bats above our slatted ceiling. Every evening they would make their exit out over the deck in a huge "whoosh." There wasn't anything to do about the situation and we learned to live with it.

It was harder to learn to live with the termites, however. They had their season to swarm and during that time we actually had to put up mosquito netting over the bed because at night, after they had dropped their wings up above the ceiling, they would crawl through the slats and drop down upon us. I just hated those squishy bugs that sometimes crawled up under the netting and would bite you.

We hadn't been in the house but three days when one of my cats disappeared while I was out in the yard with them, trying to get them acquainted with their new home. There was a fence around the yard, but it was in as dilapidated condition as the house, and Cheri found her way out a hole while I was distracted. I searched franticly for her and had all the neighbors looking too, but she appeared to be gone. I figured she had tried to head back to her home in the Philippines. Willy and I mourned her loss, laying together on the bed and crying. I cried for her, and I cried for myself too because so far I really didn't like this place. Everything and more that my friend in Kalsangi had warned me about was true and I was miserable. Here I was in this tiny town with no place to go, nothing to do, and hardly anyone to do it with. I was far away from family and there were not even telephones in that town that I could use to call home. The system was that the company office could radio to Bangkok and someone there could place a call to the United States with a

Hua Hin, Thailand

message, if needed. The difficulty of actually doing this meant that I never once in all the time we lived there called home.

Ten days later in the middle of the night, I awoke to the sound of Cheri crying outside my window. I ran to the folding front door which had way too many locks on it, and finally threw the doors open. There she was on a ledge outside the bedroom window and how she was able to determine that that room was where I would be at that time of night, I have no way of imagining. Animals certainly must have an acute sense of smell, or something. I picked her up and almost threw her over my head! This cat who had weighed a good 12 pounds, now had lost half her weight and was skin and bones – BUT ALIVE. There was great celebration that night, but for the next month it was a struggle because during the ten days that she was missing (and fighting for her life), she had gone wild and now she would not let Willy, her own brother, near her, not even in the same room. She would snarl and carry on. Willy tolerated it for a short while because he was so glad to see her, but after a while he had had enough and reciprocated. It took time, and finally peace reigned, but those two were never the good friends they had once been.

There was another night that we had an altercation, but this time with a stray cat that had come up on the front deck. I awoke to the sound of a cat fight and got out of bed to investigate, thinking my two cats were fighting again. But no, this time things were different. I saw Willy taking on this stray cat outside these floor to ceiling windows. That is a very safe way to fight, don't you think? Anyway, I didn't have any clothes on, but decided to scare that outside cat away. So I began to creep across the floor, not wanting to be naked in front of all those windows. Willy in the meantime was very intent on defending his territory and apparently did not see me, so when I reached up over his head to bang on the windows, he was so startled that he leaped up and landed on me – with all claws unsheathed! The wounds were deep, but this cat was so sorry for what he had done that I had to forgive him. The outside cat was apparently as frightened as Willy and we never had another incident like that.

We did not have to wait for long to receive our household goods because we had sent them ahead of us about four months before and the shipment was waiting for us when we arrived. As soon as I got the house set up, I was able to start building a life again, and I began to feel much better.

Once again, I got very lucky with finding a maid. She was a woman who had worked for the man that Johannes was replacing, and although she did not live in our home, she did live nearby and, of course, needed a job when we came. To my great relief, she spoke a little bit of English and that was a tremendous help to me in those early days. I wouldn't call her "conversational" in English, but she certainly was able to communicate to me and I to her. And to top it off, she was a very pleasant person who always had a smile on her face, soft spoken and unflappable. She knew the ropes of how to get about anything in that tiny town. I loved Boonyen immediately and she stayed with me the entire 10 years we lived there.

One of the first "tests" that I put Boonyen through was a party to be held in our yard for Johannes' birthday just a couple months after we arrived. This was a tradition among the agricultural department at the office that looked for any excuse to have a party. I was told that I had to prepare the food – <u>for 150 people!</u> – and they would bring the drinks. So I turned to Boonyen who had done this before and she said, "Don't worry, I will call my friends." She whipped into action, doing all the marketing on her bicycle, and spending hours with her helpers threading meat onto sticks ready to barbeque. She also made some huge pots full of a noodle dish, a rice dish and some other entrées. Every now and again, I would pop my head into the downstairs kitchen to see how it was going. I arranged for tables to be set up and a place to put the beer to cool. And that was one of the easiest parties I had ever hosted. This woman was a precious gem and she could have asked for any salary at that point.

After the first year, which was touch and go for me, I began to open my eyes to this exotic land. There were so many things to explore and I hoped we would live here long enough to do that. Little did I know that we would live here for ten years, an unheard of length of time for a family to stay in one division.

Every morning I could watch the walk at dawn of the Buddhist monks in their orange robes who would come down the beach with their begging bowls to collect rice, flowers or maybe some cigarettes from people who would go out from their homes to give their offerings. Whatever the monks collected is what they would be eating that day, and they never went hungry because Thai people really participated in their religion. These monks would return to their temples and spend the whole day praying and administering to people in need, and in the evening, I think after sundown, they could eat their one meal that day.

The temples, or "watts," were always ornate structures, painted white with gold and red trimmings. All around the rafters were placed small bells which made this wonderful sound in the wind, and were supposed to keep evil spirits away. There was always a large tray of sand at the entrance to hold the incense sticks which the locals would light. And they would buy a tiny piece of gold leaf that first would be stuck to the Buddah figure (a piece of raw garlic was used as adhesive) and then it was the tradition to place one finger on the gold leaf and then on your forehead, thus leaving a gold leaf finger print indicating that you had said your prayers. Flowers were also offered and Thailand is famous for their floral "sculptures" and leis. So, with the incense, flowers and sounds of the bells, a temple was a very fragrant place of peace.

Every temple also had its fortune teller, and I was fascinated by their particular method. They had some sort of book that went by your time, day and place of birth. When they had found that entry, this would lead them to a series of questions, which according to how you answered, would point to other questions. For instance, after I told them my time of birth, the question was asked, "Are your parents living?" A "yes" brought the question, "Are they still married?" I have always been in a quandary why if my parents were living or dead, still married or not, should that have any bearing on my future, but apparently it does. And I had to wonder, if someone else were born at exactly the same time and answered the questions in the same way, would they have the same future as me? I will probably never know the answer.

Anyway, that day this monk told me that I would have a child, a boy. This really disturbed me because I had already decided not to have children, so this would not be a good thing. I got to thinking about how the session was orchestrated and thought that perhaps it was a problem with translation of Thai to English since I had an interpreter during the interview. Maybe the word "would" should have been "could," which would make a world of difference, in my estimation. It was a question of control. So I went to another monk, this one blind and highly reputed to be very accurate. After all the initial questions and my answers, he said the <u>same thing,</u> I would have a baby boy. I said, "Wait a minute – would or could?" He fiddled with his

Hua Hin, Thailand

figures, leafed through his book and said "Could, but it would be very lucky monetarily if you would have this child." I breathed a sigh of relief and decided I didn't need the money.

My mode of transportation around Hua Hin was a bicycle. In five minutes I could ride down to the local market or just about anywhere else, since the town was so small. One problem I did have, however, was my sense of direction. My whole life I had always had a very strong sense of direction, but there was something about being in Thailand where you drive on the "wrong side of the road" that screwed up my sensor. I would get out to the main road and think, "Now, do it right this time" and I would turn right, which would be wrong almost every time. "Shoot, I did it again." I can't remember how many times this happened but it took me a very long time to be able to make a left at that corner.

The market was the usual Third World dirty, smelly place that I had come to know from Costa Rica and Davao. I learned not to walk down certain alleys that had fish or chickens because the stench was overwhelming. In Thailand there was another area that I avoided too and that was where they had all these cockroaches on sticks, ready for barbeque. I think they were some kind of a water bug, but they looked like large roaches to me. But the dried squid area was far and away the worst. The fishermen would lay their catch of squid out on racks in the sun to dry and the smell reminded me of that old paper mill smell combined with dirty feet and maybe burning rubber. That smell is burned into my memory because right next to my house there on the beach was a squid drying operation and when the wind was coming from that direction during one season of the year, I literally had to leave the house.

But when you got past all of that mess, the market was still a very interesting place to find treasurers. There was always the store selling baskets (as if I needed more), and then there were these gorgeous "klong jars," which I will talk about later.

During mango season of each year there was a special treat that I will never forget. Hua Hin was apparently famous for it and that was sticky rice. This one woman, whose recipe surpassed all others, would set up her stall on the street and she would have a large basin of sticky rice, neatly covered with plastic wrap to keep the flies off. Then there was a basket full of lovely ripe mangos. You would specify how many grams you wanted and she would weigh out and place that amount in a plastic bag. Then she would peel and cut up a mango and place that in the bag too, closing the bag with a rubber band so you could easily carry it over your finger. Most anything you bought to eat on the street was placed in a plastic bag with a rubber band. Even soft drinks with ice were dispensed in this manner so there was no empty bottle to discard later.

Now try as I might, I could never pass up her stall when I went to market. Indeed there were times when that was the whole reason for going to market in the first place. So I would buy my bag of sticky rice and head home, but I could never wait and would start to eat it even while riding the bike. I was totally addicted. The trouble with it was that this big bag of sticky rice would all land in your stomach in one large lump and give you a good stomach ache, but that was no deterrent to doing it all over again as soon as possible. After all, the season did not last very long and then the opportunity was gone for tasting this marvelous treat until the next year.

I did my best to stock all our usual foods in my pantry and this was always a challenge due to the necessity of doing the major part of my grocery shopping in Bangkok once a month. Because I was still baking all our own bread, I had to calculate the amount of flour to buy to make our one month

Hua Hin, Thailand

supply of bread, mainly sandwich rolls for my husband's lunch. These would be stored in the freezer. If I would be leaving on a home visit, which usually lasted one month or six weeks, I had to stock the freezer with enough to last the whole time. In fact, I would also cook all his meals and have them individually wrapped as well. Every cranny of space was utilized. Boonyen would then be responsible for heating up a package and cooking whatever vegetables to complete the meal. We had it down to a science.

I even tried my hand at making preserves. My favorite was orange marmalade made during the season when you could get nice oranges. But one year it went terribly wrong. The recipe goes that you have to cook the mixture of oranges and sugar down to a thick consistency, which takes a long time over low heat. I busied myself with another project during this time, and, you guessed it, totally forgot about the pot on the stove. By the time I starting smelling the smoke, it was much too late. Racing into the kitchen, I found it had completely boiled over and I now had about one inch of goo down inside all the burners. I never was able to entirely clean it up.

In the first year of living in Thailand I resisted learning the language because, "dah," it was an incredibly difficult thing to contemplate. I already knew that languages did not come easily to me, so the idea that I could even begin to learn Thai was ridiculous. But the company had provided a teacher for whomever wanted to take classes, so I thought I could at least try. We would start out with lesson number one and maybe get through two or three. Then this teacher, who was also a secretary at the office, would get busy and have to cancel class, or I would take a trip away from home. When we managed to get back together we would begin at lesson one again. And so it went. Finally we had progressed through lesson twelve, a real feat, I can tell you, but that was the last. From there on I was on my own. By this time I had enough Thai under my hat to be able to go to market, knew my numbers and money, knew my colors, sizes (big and small), could get a taxi in Bangkok and find a bathroom ("Yu tee nai hong nam?" if you ever travel there). This, coupled with a belief that we would probably not stay too many years in that division and once you leave Thailand the chances are slim of ever using the language anywhere else, was a good reason to quit lessons. And that is one of my regrets, that I did not learn the language enough to be conversational, and therefore it was a brick wall between me and getting to know people.

I remember one of the first words that I was able to read in Thai. We were traveling down the road on a trip to Bangkok and there was this big tanker truck ahead of us. With nothing better to do, I tried to make out a word written on the back of the truck. First you have to figure out the consonants and then attack the vowels which are placed above, below, in front or back of a consonant. The placement of the vowel then determines the "tone" of the word, and there are five tones. Also the same word in each of the five tones had a different meaning. (Are you getting any sense at all of how difficult this language is?) So I had figured out the word as "wai fai" but had no idea the meaning. The driver clued me in that it meant "flammable," which of course would be written on a tanker. My next word was a bit easier. Again we were going down the highway and I had time to read some letters on a truck ahead of us. It started out "I" and then, "S," "KR," "EE," "M." Did you get it? <u>Ice Cream</u> – apparently pronounced the same in both languages. I felt triumphant.

One day I was a little late for class, but I had such a good excuse. You see, I was out "shooting elephants." I had gotten on

Hua Hin, Thailand

my bicycle to ride over to the club house for my Thai class when suddenly I saw walking towards me this huge elephant. I quickly rode back to my house to get my camera and then took off down the street to get some pictures. Where I came from it was not the usual thing to see an elephant walking down your street, so here was a photo op that I could not miss. I tracked that beast down through some back streets of the town and watched as the handler was asking for offerings. When I finally got to class and gave them my excuse for my tardiness, the teacher did not even bat an eye. Life in the Third World, I guess.

Since there was no television, no newspapers or radio to listen to except the local Thai versions, no malls or other shopping, of course, no movies either, a good company wife had to entertain herself somehow. I thought myself very fortunate to be an artist who could always find some creative thing to do. It was great fun to find local materials that then could be made into something beautiful, and it's amazing the things you can come up with if you put your mind to it.

As soon as my house was in order, I began to do batik paintings with dyes that I had shipped from Davao. Sometimes I would have three or four going at the same time and I worked between my upstairs kitchen and downstairs kitchen. All the waxing was done close to my stove upstairs and the dying and really messy part downstairs. Soon a Thai girl, Pom, one of the secretaries at the office who lived nearby, became my apprentice and she would come over on weekends. We would both be hunched over our project, painting hot wax on to cloth with the "tjanting" tool. This was a small metal cup with a spout on the end of a bamboo stick. One day we decided to bake some bread at the same time – she had never done this before and wanted to learn. After all the kneading and such we popped it into the oven and then began our waxing during the baking period. Do you know that we forgot completely about that baking bread right under our noses and didn't "wake up" until it began to smoke! Only a true artist could be so engrossed in their project to not even notice burning bread!

It was somewhere along in this period of time that Johannes and I took a trip to Indonesia, touring Jakarta, JoJakarka and the countryside. A side trip to Borobordour, an ancient temple, was fascinating. But, for me, the highlight of the whole vacation were several trips to batik factories in the area. I was determined to learn what kind of dyes they were using and almost all of the businesses used a German dye which I knew was available in Bangkok. The conditions for the workers at these factories was absolutely deplorable. You would see small children working under a hole in the roof for light, making these intricate designs with the tjanting tool. It gave me a whole new appreciation of a piece of batik fabric for sale in the market.

With the name of that dye in hand, I looked up the company there in Bangkok and was given the location of some retailers down in Chinatown. The company driver took me around, and we found one small shop that specialized in batik equipment and dyes. I was a kid in a candy store. It was a tiny place, dark and dusty, with a little old Chinese woman manning the counter. You would place your order for whatever colors you wanted and then she would go into the back room to fill the order from larger bins. These were excellent quality dye powders which you had to mix with several chemicals, but the results were color fast. This allowed me to begin making clothing which could be laundered.

After several times of buying dyes at this store in Chinatown, I went in there one day to get my usual supply. I had red, yellow and orange on the list, but then decided, since orange was a bit expensive, that I would just make do by mixing

Hua Hin, Thailand

red and yellow to get my orange, so I asked the clerk to scratch off the orange color from my list. When she returned from the back room, the whole order was wrapped up and ready to go, so I paid my money and went on my merry way. Now an order of dyes would last me several months so I did not have to go there every time I went to Bangkok. After that particular trip when we had made our two hour journey back to Hua Hin, I unwrapped my package of dyes and found that orange had been included in the order. Then I looked at my receipt and realized that I had not paid for it. There was only one thing I could do. I would wait for my next trip three months down the road to pay for the dye. And so at that time I went back to see the little old Chinese woman, but only speaking market Thai, I knew I was not getting through to her what had taken place. She had this incredulous look on her face, like what ARE you talking about. Finally I knew there was no hope of ever explaining things and I just placed the money on the desk and walked out. I know I made her day, this crazy "farang" (foreign) lady just walking in and placing money on the table. I bet she thought, "This is my lucky day!" and went right out to play the lottery.

Since I could now begin to make clothing with batik and tie-dye, it was a whole new adventure and I began to make T-shirts. My friend Pom joined me and we were having a blast. One year I was going to be returning to visit family both in Holland and the United States and decided to make T-shirts for everyone. Pom had her own list of gifts she wanted to make. After we had taken a dozen or so out of the last boil out pot on the stove, every one a masterpiece, Pom had the idea that we should go into business. There was a small tourist trade in town and it seemed a great idea to try cornering some of their baht (money). So began our business which we called "Conversationals." We put some down in the local gift shops of hotels in town, but also we began, by word of mouth, to get orders from people working at the company for our product. They would say, "I want to have a red T-shirt with flowers on the right shoulder," and we could make it up for them. We were getting so many orders that I put my maid to work also to help.

It was a time in my life when I felt I needed to make a change. That translated in my mind as it would be great to have some plastic surgery done on my nose. Thailand was the perfect place to do this because they had first class physicians and they were cheap. I did a little research and found a man in Bangkok with a reputation of being the best plastic surgeon in the region. Since a very young age, maybe ten years old, I had been aware of this hump in my nose that made a very unattractive profile and the doctor agreed that he could fix that and suggested also that I have a chin implant which would further correct the profile. I also wanted to have an old scar on my forehead filed down.

This would be the first time in my life to be put under anesthesia and I was a bit worried about that, but not enough to stop me. The day arrived and I remember that wonderful feeling of going under. I thought I could smell mangos and then was out. I came to in the middle of the night, there in that Bangkok clinic, and called the nurse in because I felt sick. Then I proceeded to vomit blood all over the floor because she wasn't fast enough with a pan. I could tell she was scared because she was alone on the ward. I just went right back to sleep. The next day I saw myself in the mirror and then I got scared. My whole face was bandaged, bruised and a war zone. The nose was swollen to twice normal size. What had I done! Could I possibly heal to anything resembling normal?

After several days there at the clinic, it was time to check out and return to Hua Hin. I wanted to have as few bandages as possible, so the doctor said the nurse could remove the large

Hua Hin, Thailand

chin bandage and just put something smaller. But to do this she grabbed hold of one end and just ripped it off in one swift yank. My God, I thought she had torn my whole face off.

A company driver was supposed to meet me at the clinic, but, for whatever reason, that did not happen and they called and told me to get a taxi to this hotel and from there I could hire another taxi to take me all the way to my home. I was horrified, because this meant that I would have to spend at least some time in public with these awful bandages and bruised face. There was no other way, so I did it. In the back of the taxi I sort of hunched down to hide my face and spent a very long day getting home.

Once there I had to deal with my husband and my curious neighbors. Johannes, of course, knew what I had done, because he had to pay for it. If he was shocked at my appearance, he made no comment. But I had told a little bit different story to my neighbors. I told them only that I was having this forehead scar resurfaced and that my face might be swollen and bruised as a result. It was my intension that nobody was going to see me for at least a week. However, a curious neighbor just barged right into my kitchen, nothing I could do about it. I still did not fess up to the total extent of my reconstruction and I did not tell anyone in my family for many years. In fact, my own mother went to her grave never knowing. This was because I always looked so much like my mother that I thought I would offend her by revealing a nose job. My own husband who knew me best, or one hopes, thought it was a waste of money because he could not see any difference. But for me, I felt a world of change and have never regretted the procedure.

There was another occasion for me to be in a hospital in Bangkok. I was having trouble with painful spasms in the chest and the company doctor wanted me to go in to have a whole series of tests run. It meant an overnight at the hospital. I learned that there was another company person there at the same time, Stanley, who was a large man who enjoyed his beer and had the figure to prove it. I started out with the usual blood work and a stress test and then they wanted to check some internal organs which required that I drink a large glass of barium. You remember that white chalky nasty stuff. Well, I have a problem to swallow <u>anything</u> that is even slightly disagreeable so for me to swallow that barium was a feat worth noting. My throat just wanted to close up, but I tried hard. They kept saying, "Drink a little faster, drink a little faster," and I would manage another gulp. They seemed at last satisfied and it was interesting to watch the monitor and see my insides. By late afternoon I was finished for the day and decided to pay Stanley a visit. We got to talking about our various tests and he said he was going to have the same barium test the next day.

At a brief consultation the next morning, I learned that I had a hiatal hernia. The doctor literally walked in the door, told me I had a "hole in my stomach," handed me a big wad of antacid tablets, and walked out. I was stunned! A Hole in My Stomach? I was doomed to eat 20 antacid tablets before every meal? I couldn't cope with this news, so after returning to Hua Hin, we sent all my results to the head medical office of the company in San Francisco, and the recommendation was that I begin some sort of exercise program that would strengthen the diaphragm. I threw away all those antacids and took up running.

About one month later, Stanley and his wife Wannee were giving a dinner party at their home and he told his side of the story. At the hospital the day after I visited him in his room, he went in for his barium test. When they handed him this large glass of barium, he just tossed it back like chugging a beer. He was remembering what I said that the nurses had told me to

Hua Hin, Thailand

drink it fast. They then handed him another glass which was dispatched similarly. By the third glass they got what they needed. Stanley said he returned home and didn't go to the bathroom for a week, and then he had to break it up with a stick to get the toilet to flush! AND IT WAS ALL MY FAULT! I still can't tell this story without shedding tears of laughter.

We had been with Dole Foods Company for about 12 years now and I had taken on the role of hostess, entertaining visiting company wives. A car and driver were always provided for me to take the ladies around town and the countryside, and more or less keep them out of the hair of their men while they were touring the plantation. A must on the women's tour would be a trip to the "klong" jar factories in a neighboring city. A klong jar was a large ceramic urn used to collect rain water in the old days and still used today for that purpose or, in my case, filled with ice to cool the beer. These factories were amazing places where you could walk around to watch the people producing these wonderful jars. There were the clay pits where the mud was processed to just the right degree of stickiness by people mushing it with their feet. I could stand for long times watching the next guy who was forming the pots on a wheel that was kicked manually by another person who would hang on to a rope suspended from the ceiling. The kiln was a huge mound that could fit hundreds of jars inside at one time. There was another area where, after the first firing, designs were applied. The most popular was a dragon wrapped around the side, and this was applied with just a thumb in a matter of one minute. After touring the factory, we would end up in the show room where we women could shop for pieces that we <u>needed</u> to have.

Besides these places which made klong jars, there were also "blue and white" ceramic factories which were just down the road, so they would be our next stop. Sometimes as you walked around in those places, you would see children sitting there painting the designs and you would have to wonder how, at such young ages, they were able to paint such sophisticated pictures. The reason I have such a large collection of blue and white is because I think I must have bought something every time I went there.

One factory was indeed the highlight of any tour and that was to the one that was producing "antiques" for the world market. The "front" was just a fish sauce jar factory, but the daughter of the owner worked for our company, so we were allowed into a back area where the "real" work was going on. Here you would find gorgeous ceramic statues of old Chinese style, huge blue and white vessels, and many Ming Dynasty items. Everything was sitting around in the dirt and dust during their aging process. Sometimes a piece would also be buried for a while or an acid used to antique it. At times you would see in a display case an authentic Ming bowl which was being copied. My advise to anyone who wants to collect antique ceramics, you better know your stuff because these people were good.

On our way back to Hua Hin from there, sometimes we would stop at a city just north of us where there was an old palace of one of the previous kings of Thailand. This was the king portrayed in the movie "Anna and the King of Siam," or "The King and I." It is interesting that that movie was banned in Thailand for many, many years because it was thought that the king was put in a very negative light. Apparently, a school teacher from England did actually spend some time in Thailand teaching, but she would never have been given the prominence or privileges that Debra Kerr was given. It just didn't happen, much less the implied attraction between her and the king.

Anyway, this palace sits up on top of a high hill with very flat land for miles around. You have to walk up many stairs

Hua Hin, Thailand

and avoid being accosted by the hundreds of monkeys which inhabit that hill to reach the top. From there you can see why the site was chosen. There is a lovely breeze and the view is spectacular of rice paddies as far as the eye could see. The palace was, of course, very ornate befitting a king, but was not really very large. It was a series of individual rooms with courtyards between them. The king's main palace was in Bangkok, so this would have been just a vacation home.

A must for any visitor to Thailand was, of course, the floating market. When I accompanied visitors on this trip, we had to spend a night in Bangkok because these attractions were just outside that city. Our driver would drop us off at a pier where we would step onto long tail boats, called this because of their special motors which had long shafts for the propellers to navigate through waters clogged with floating water hyacinths. Then we would begin to travel along canals just busting with activities. We could watch people in their homes along the water doing their laundry, taking baths, or brushing their teeth, all in a river filled with all manner of pollution. There were temples along the way to add bright spots of color and many markets selling local wares. Instead of street vendors with small carts, there were small boats that would come along side ours and offer fruits or vegetables. This was truly an adventure where you would learn about the local culture of this land.

Back at home, a tour of Hua Hin was also on the menu, if for no other reason than to give the guest an idea of our every day lives. We would go down to the market and walk around in a temple and maybe have lunch at a restaurant called "Charie's Brown" where you could actually eat in an upstairs air conditioned room.

One day as I was about to leave my house with a guest, we headed out my door and she exclaimed to me, "Wow, what's that?" I looked up to where she was pointing and said my own explicative. There high up in a royal palm tree was this gigantic wasp nest. It must have been at least three feet in diameter, and it was hanging down right over my gate. The wasps had constructed it while all the palm fronds were pointed up, but with time these fronds dry up, bend down, and eventually fall off the palm. Here this thing was, hanging like a black cloud right over my gate and ready to fall. I couldn't waste a moment so I ran back into the house and called our company office to send someone out to do something. Within half an hour a man arrived, machete in hand, I think with the idea to just climb up that palm and cut the thing down. But he took one look at the size of the nest and scrapped that idea. Plan B: smoke the wasps out. That evening, while the insects were all home and quiet for the night, a crew arrived and lit a torch on the end of a long pole. I could see what they had in mind, but I was not very happy with the safety issue. This palm was fairly close to my very old house, and the garden hose didn't begin to have the pressure necessary to reach that high. But since there was no Plan C, they set the nest on fire. Quickly the whole top of the palm was ablaze and then the concern was the embers flying everywhere, including my roof. There were some tense moments, but my house and I survived.

Every year the royal family of Thailand would come to spend time at their summer palace in Hua Hin, just a short walk down the beach from my house. You couldn't, however, actually walk past the palace while the family was in residence. During their approximate two month stay, they would visit all their projects in the area. One of these projects was a dam being built on the edge of our company's pineapple plantation which would provide much needed water to the farmers in the area. Since some of Dole's land would be under water soon, the company donated that land to the king. So there was to be a

Hua Hin, Thailand

grand ceremony to dedicate this new dam, and most of the royal family would there, the king, queen and two of their daughters. There were tents set up to protect everyone from the blistering sun, and they had tried to lay down some gravel in the muddy terrain. Our folding chairs still gave you that "sinking feeling" that you were going to tip over backward.

I was chosen to represent the company in presenting flowers to the queen, so I tried to dress appropriately with a dress with sleeves and I was also wearing high heels (foolish in hindsight in that mud). I had brought along my camera for this special occasion, but handed it to my husband when I got in the receiving line for the queen. Then at last the royal family arrived and got out of their vehicle very sensibly dressed for the occasion with pant suits, umbrella and boots. The queen began to go down the line of greeters from the town and I was last in line. I was holding a special tray on which were placed a bouquet of flowers because I was not supposed to touch the queen. She would just pick up the offering from each person and hand it to her assistant behind her. Then it was my turn. I did the required curtsy; the queen accepted my flowers, and suddenly she began to speak to me. Now, she had not spoken to anyone else and I had not been warned of this so was totally unprepared. My heart was thumping so loudly I am sure she could see my nervousness. But this truly elegant lady spoke to me in a soft lovely British English. She asked my name and how I liked Thailand and then commented on the beauty of the countryside. It was truly a thrilling moment in my life.

My roll of film was used up so I tried to rewind it (remember life before digitals?), but something was not right. So I went to a camera shop in town where they could open the camera in the dark room. To my great dismay, THERE WAS NO FILM IN THE CAMERA. Fortunately for me, there were many cameras operating that day and I was able to get a wonderful photo of my presentation of flowers to the queen. I sent that photo to my mother in Florida and she promptly had it put in the town paper where it hit the front page. In that quiet little town, they were probably desperate for something interesting to print.

During my first few years of living in Thailand, I was excited to explore this exotic land. With that aim, another company wife, Alma, and I joined the Siam Cultural Society. Every year they made several trips around Thailand and surrounding countries with the intention of studying the histories and how they intertwined. The first trip we took with them was to the neighbor to the west called Burma in those days. Today the name is Myanmar. Now I had thought I was living in a place that was not yet in the twentieth century, but stepping off the plane in Rangoon was going back in time two centuries. Our group of about 27 people were some of the first tourists allowed to come in after the communist rulers opened their doors. We could choose between a 24 hour stay or an 8 day stay, that was it. And we were monitored closely, only allowed to exchange money in government offices, and were not allowed to travel by train, only plane, from one place to another because they were interested in extracting as many dollars as possible from us. We were assigned a Burmese tour guide to keep us on the approved path. Her name was Pansie, a very pretty young woman. Our first day we spent touring that city with its wonderful old temples. This was a country, before the communists took over, that practiced a very pure version of Buddhism, unlike Thailand which has mixed in some Hindu rituals. With both our own tour guide and Pansie, we were being lectured about all the old kings and the connected histories of Burma and Siam, and my friend Alma and I soon "spaced out" on it all. There was no way we were going to understand or

Hua Hin, Thailand

remember those names which were half a page long. So we would quietly excuse ourselves from the pack and go outside the temple to the market. There was always a market at the side of a temple, being the gathering place of the community, and there in Burma all the products were local, unlike Thailand which displayed products from around the world. But we were interested only in the local wares anyway, so we were fascinated by the hats, baskets and beggar bowls that the monks used. Our only concern was finding space in our luggage if we bought something.

From Rangoon we flew to Mandalay (you know, where the flying fishes play) and we boarded a barge to look at more temples up the river. We had to just sit on a wooden floor but at least we had a roof over our heads because it began to rain. This, however, produced a wonderful memory that I treasure. As we progressed up that river in the gentle rain, the surrounding banks became a watercolor painting of tones of greens and grays. A sailboat came by with a tall rust colored sail and made a perfect photo.

Our next stop was to Inlay Lake where we would be boarding boats to watch an annual Buddhist ceremony where they would be transporting a Buddah image from one community along the lake to another. Many towns were built out _in_ the lake, with the houses up on stilts. They even did their farming in a unique way on that lake by tacking long woven matts with bamboo poles to the bottom of the lake, piling dirt on top of them and then planting their vegetables. Harvesting was all done in small boats pulled up to the side of the matt.

Our group was divided into about four boats and we started to follow the procession. The main float was a huge thing in the shape of a golden bird. On the top, or back, of the bird was a pagoda that housed the Buddah image which looked like just a large lump of gold from having been rubbed with gold leaf for so many years. The golden bird would stop at towns built along the edges of the lake where there would be a temple, and the Buddah would be carried in a solemn procession to rest for one night in that temple, thereby blessing it. Of course, all the local people were out in their finest dress which was an ankle length sarong for both men and women.

After several hours of our being out in that boat, we all needed a rest stop and that would be this tea house out in the middle of the lake. We all disembarked and climbed up to find wonderful little bowls of tea waiting for us. And then the line formed for the bathroom at the back of the house. After each person entered, he would exit with this big smile on his/her face and even be laughing. Everyone wanted to know why the smile? No one would reveal the secret, you had to find out yourself. Finally it was my turn. The toilet was, of course, just a hole in the center of the room and as you looked down through that hole the sun was striking the water and you could see right down to the bottom of the lake. And what you saw was a beautiful aquarium of fish into which you were peeing. It had to bring a smile to your face.

When we finished spending three days on the boats following the procession from town to town, and before we left the area, we went to a local market because several of us had expressed a wish to buy some of that wonderful tea we had been served. So Pansie lead the way. There were all the usual local wares displayed on blankets on the ground or in small stalls. It began to rain and, not having an umbrella with me, I decided to head into a covered area to see if I could find one. I was so pleased to find the stall selling the special red umbrellas that you would see the monks carrying through the streets while they did their morning begging. It would serve two purposes, to keep the

Hua Hin, Thailand

rain off and as a lovely souvenir to bring home. I immediately opened it and went walking outside through the market. I began to notice that people were pointing and laughing at me, but I was keeping dry in the rain, so I did not let that deter me. When I arrived back at the bus, Pansie also began to laugh and clued me in that I was using an umbrella that only a male monk would use. OK, at least it appeared that I was not offending them because they were all laughing and didn't seem upset.

As we traveled through the countryside to find yet another temple, the scenery had the most amazing colors. The soil was rich red, the sky very blue with a puffy white cloud here and there, and scattered over the whole area were the ruins of small temples, some of them still showing a bit of white paint. You apparently earn more points in heaven by building a new temple rather than repairing an old one. There were thousands of temples in all stages of decay, from slightly to just a pile of bricks. We stayed at a government guest house that night and in the morning headed into town to a large temple with some important history. Alma and I by now were known as the shoppers and the tour guide knew where to find us.

I had not felt very good that morning and questioned if I should even board the bus, but I didn't want to miss anything so decided to go. Big Mistake. As soon as we arrived at our destination, I said to Pansie, I need to find a bathroom and quickly. She lead me down to the market and a person there guided me out behind where the latrines were set up. They were like little houses built up on stilts and you climbed a ladder to enter. But you could see what was under each latrine and that was a hole dug into the ground, all completely filled with you know what and covered with green flies. I took one look, turned around and found Pansie, who arranged for a taxi to take me back to the guest house. Now here's the great part. This taxi was a horse and cart and I sat on a wooden bench in the back. We went clippity-clopping down the road through this tranquil countryside for about ten miles. I really don't know how I managed to survive that trip. I was torn between two feelings, enjoying the view, but really wishing the ride were smoother and the horse would go faster.

At one of our last stops, Alma and I were able to teach something to Pansie about tourists. She was always amazed at the things we were interested to buy, not understanding this thing about adding to our collections of baskets and hats. We made our usual exit to the market and discovered a stall selling hand woven rugs. The upright loom was even set up nearby for us to watch as the person would grab handfuls of raw, unspun wool and weave them into the weft. The final products were hanging out front in their natural colors of brown and cream. Our eyes just latched right on to the display but the problem was to haggle the price, so we went to find Pansie. When she saw what it was we wanted to buy, she asked why in the world would we want to buy one of those carpets? We assured her that they were a wonderful souvenir that any tourist would love to buy. So in the future she could bring tourists to that stall and get her little commission for doing so. We hope we opened her eyes.

Another trip we took with the Siam Cultural Society was to the northern regions of Thailand, to Chiang Mai and the area known as the Golden Triangle. This time it was a group of about 80 people and we filled two large buses. The journey from Bangkok took about 10 hours on the train, so we arrived late in the day and enjoyed our first night at a nice hotel. The next day we headed north in the two buses to see the poppy fields that spread over an area where Laos, Burma and Thailand intersect, the Golden Triangle. The poppies are grown on the Thai side

Hua Hin, Thailand

and the sap is smuggled over the border to Burma where it is processed into heroin. Then it again returns to Thailand and makes its way out and across the world.

Here we were, two huge buses of tourists walking out into the fields of poppies, watching people there harvest the sap from these flower pods. The tour guide was walking back and forth along our lines and saying, "Please don't pick any pods or put any seeds in your pocket." The reason being, of course, that the possession of either could land you in prison – a place you definitely didn't want to be. But it was very interesting to watch the workers scrape the sap from the pods with a knife and cut perhaps old pods off and toss them into a large basket on their backs which they held with a band around their forehead.

I knew immediately that I needed to have one of those baskets for my collection, so I approached a girl and asked her how much she would spend for that basket in the market. I paid her a little bit more and we were both happy. Before carrying it away, however, I shook the basket out and checked for any remaining seeds or pods. You can't be too careful.

Along the way the Siam Cultural Society made its required stop at a temple in that area. It was built on top of a hill in an area of many "bon bon" type hills. It was the custom to remove your shoes before climbing to the top of the hill and since there were no restrooms up there, we were all advised to use the "facilities" near the parking lot, boys to the left and girls to the right. And here is yet another latrine story. We women headed down a path into the woods to the right and were soon climbing up a neighboring hill. This lead to the so called restroom which amounted to a small tin shed hanging out over the edge of the hill. When you opened the door you were confronted with two horizontal polls supported by two vertical polls. You had to balance yourself over these polls, which looked so fragile and dangerous that most women continued on around the bend into the woods, preferring a well established bush on the hillside.

The absolute highlight of this trip was an evening event. Our tour guide knew the chief of a tribe up in the hills and we, as a group, were invited to a wedding that would take place that night. A whole case of rubber flip-flop shoes was purchased for the tribe and we also all threw some money into a pot. These were brought as wedding gifts from our group. We left after dark, all carrying flashlights because we were going off into the wilderness and there would be no lights. The last mile or so we had to manage on foot as best we could, carefully picking our way down a path with our flashlights, hoping that the infamous cobra snakes were not hunting in our area.

Once at the village, it was on top of a hill and all the homes were thatched roofed huts. There was a huge fire which had been lit in the center, the only source of light. This made for wonderful photography because everyone and everything was washed in this glow from the fire, and the background was pitch black. People were dressed in their finest which were made of a black cloth ornately embroidered in many colors. The women all wore hats and you could tell by the style if she was married or not.

We guests sat on logs around the edge of the circle and as the ceremony began, the women formed a ring around the fire and began to dance. The music from flutes and drums was punctuated by stomping of feet in the dust which would send up a little cloud. Later it was the men's turn and they were a bit more rowdy than the women. At last it was decided that this couple was now married and our gifts were presented. Food, of course, was offered to everyone, but I was glad I had already eaten my dinner.

Hua Hin, Thailand

The next day we attended another festival and watched as elephants played soccer on a large field. We also had an opportunity to ride one of these animals through the forest for a ways and it was fun to watch them getting their bath in a stream.

Chiang Mai has a huge craft industry with surrounding villages that specialize in one craft or another. There is the umbrella making area where you can watch paper umbrellas being hand painted. Then there are communities that only do wood carving. Another excels in working with silver, making jewelry mainly. The weaving village, of course, fascinated me.

There was one unbelievable place where some Belgium nuns had come to Thailand many years before and had taught bobbin lace work to a group of blind people. You would not believe what these people could do without eyesight. The work was intricate and beautiful, lovely matting for pictures, or collar and cuffs for a blouse. Truly amazing.

When my niece Jill was 15 years old, she came to spend the summer with me. This would be the first time I became aware of how old I looked. I was going along in life feeling pretty young and frisky, and then this teenager came to stay and something changed. You remember that I did not have kids so had no idea how to entertain one. So we would go down to the market to explore and local vendors would look at the two of us and guess that she was <u>my daughter</u>. What? You mean I look old enough to have a 15 year old child? It was a cruel awakening. But we were having so much fun together that these feelings soon were forgotten. I introduced her to the world of batik and she helped in the little business Pom and I had going.

I had been asked, through my friend Pom's boyfriend, to give some English classes to the border patrol men who were slated to go to the border of Malaysia where English was spoken. We perhaps had one real class and the rest of the time was spent on outings. So while Jill was visiting, we went with the men out to an island just south of town called "the sleeping lion," where they would be doing some scuba diving exams. We boarded some rubber pontoon boats to get there and upon arriving at the beach, to our absolute delight, it was not sand but covered with rocks. Jill and I were big rock hounds, so the moment our feet touched solid ground, we began to collect rocks. These were no ordinary rocks, but due to their makeup of layers of different types of rock, each rock had a picture on it from different colored layers eroding away. I found one with a picture of Don Quixote and Sancho Panza riding through a mountain pass – no kidding. Jill found one of a sailboat on water sailing past a rocky cliff. We made piles of rocks along the beach to be collected later for transporting home. It was possible that we were going to sink the boats to get home, but we insisted that every rock be taken. Jill, of course, had to throw out many that she had collected because at the end of the summer she had to fly home and lift her suitcase in the process.

Jill, Pom, another boyfriend (French) and I also made a trip to Chiang Mai, this time taking the night train from Bangkok. It began at six in the evening and took 12 hours. Each seat folded down into a bed for sleeping, and it wasn't long in that tropical country for night to descend. About that time a big thunder storm came up and Jill and I sat mesmerized by the display of lightning out our window. There was hardly a moment that wasn't almost like daylight.

In Chiang Mai we did all the tourist things one does there and just had a great time. Using Pom as our translator, we were able to learn a wider range of things to do on our own and didn't have to book an expensive tour to do it.

Hua Hin, Thailand

Finally it was Jill's time to return home and I felt much older but wiser too. Isn't it a good thing to "mother" a teenager and then be able to send her home?

Our old friends, Edna and Walter, came over to visit too, and it was during that time that I began to think about having some nice wooden furniture made. All my friends were going into Bangkok to the furniture makers and having wonderful housefuls of things brought down. I felt it was my turn, so Edna and I made a trip to Bangkok to take a look. This particular factory used teak wood for everything and produced a modern style of knock-down designs with leather upholstery. I decided on a living room set of a sofa, two chairs, a coffee table and two side tables. You could order the basic version or the deluxe. My dear friend Edna keep saying to me, "Go ahead, Carol, you deserve it," so I keep adding more and more pieces to my order, upgrading as I went along. By the time I had finished and they added up the bill, I had spent about $3000. Now I began to get just a bit worried about returning home to my husband who could easily live on orange crates. I put the blame squarely on Edna with all her encouragement.

Hua Hin was beginning to change and the tourist industry was starting to return. The old beach house I had been living in was in the way of progress and was going to be torn down to build a new condo unit. So I had to find another home. One of the company houses on the north side of town, again on the beach, became available and I jumped at the offer because I had always liked it, in spite of being away from the center of town. This was a newer and larger home with three bedrooms, three bathrooms, and living area upstairs and dining room, bathroom and huge lanai downstairs. The kitchen was in a separate building, as was the custom since the maids usually did all the cooking. But in my case, I wanted a kitchen inside the main house, so I had one built more or less under the staircase that lead to the second floor. I would have loved to have a large window to the outside, but, hey, I was happy to be able to get a glass of water during the night and not go outside to do it.

This home had a huge garden which needed lots of work, so it was at this point that I took up gardening. Now I don't mean just planting a few flowers here and there. No, I mean hauling rocks from the vacant lot next door to build a large rock garden between the main house and the maid's quarters. This was a mud patch when I came with one half dead cactus and a large tree in the middle of this 12 foot by 12 foot area. I brought in enough rocks to cover the area and then planted green things in between the rocks. My main reason for all the rocks was to prevent my dog from immediately digging up anything I might put in the ground.

Then in the large front yard I decided on a Japanese style entry area. A previous occupant of the home had brought in one very large rock and set it between three palms, apparently when the trees were young. Now the palms had grown to giant size and swallowed the rock. I wanted to rescue it from that space and move it to a place of glory in my Japanese garden. To do this I called in some help from the company gardeners. A crew of three men came over and when they took one look at that big rock and heard where I wanted to place it, they almost rolled on the ground in laughter. They did, however, manage to humor me and after much effort, they placed the rock in its perfect place to be appreciated by everyone entering that house. Along with the rock I had some stepping stones set into a truck load of gravel and put some plants along the side of the lanai. To this was added a bird bath which would also serve as a water bowl to my dog.

Hua Hin, Thailand

One of my treasured memories is of the day I was sitting down in my lanai enjoying my nice garden when a movement caught my eye. At first I thought it was the ordinary black and white bird that you saw often in the yard at the birdbath, but on closer observation I saw this magnificent bird with a very long tail which had a plume on the end. He could flick this plume up and down and he was enjoying his bath immensely. I ran for my bird book and learned it was a magpie, which was usually found in fields where they would hunt for seeds, but here by the ocean he was definitely out of his territory. But it was one of those things which you never forget, just the beauty of that moment.

As long as we are on the subject of critters, here is a story that I feel is very unique. I know there can't be many people in the world who can claim to have had experienced this. In this two story house there were balconies outside the bedrooms, and near one was a tree that would at times begin to hang over and touch the railing. This became a highway for ants to enter the house, so I would inspect it periodically and cut the tree back. As I came out onto the balcony that day to do the pruning, I noticed the shed skin of a snake hanging in the branches. I took my hand to flick it off and to my surprise, the skin was still attached to the snake, whom I am sure was equally as surprised as I was. It started to make a beeline back down the tree as fast as he could under the circumstances, having a human holding on to his old skin, and the feeling it made to me was like when you slowly tear off a band-aid, pop, pop, pop. At last he was free and I was left with an empty snake skin but also a great memory and story.

This story reminds me of another that took place on that same balcony. I used to step out there in the early mornings because it had a lovely view of the ocean. This one time, however, a sudden gust of wind blew the door closed behind me, and I found myself locked out. In assessing my situation, I was alone and barefoot on a second story balcony. My husband was at work and I couldn't contact him anyway. It was the maid's day off. The only tall plant close enough to reach was way too weak to support my weight. I had only one option and that was to slide down the rain spout, so that is what I did. Then it was a matter of cutting the screen on the locked kitchen door to get back into the house. At this point I finally learned to hide a key outside the house, which would not have helped me up there on that balcony, but since "Murphy" seemed to be rattling my cage, it seemed a wise decision.

The ants in that yard were something to be feared. They would paste leaves together and make nests for themselves and there would be thousands of these large red insects with jaws the size of crabs. One day I was out there doing my morning gardening, cleaning under some bushes and did not notice the nest until too late. A swarm began running up my arm and by the time I could get them off, I had been bitten at least 50 times. The hives began to move up my arm and over my body with such speed that I couldn't even get into the house before I was covered. Getting to the doctor was not easy either since I only had a bicycle, lived at least 5 miles from town, and the company doctor was usually out at the plantation 20 miles away. It was faster to just call a friend to help me out. Most people, especially those with kids, had a virtual pharmacy in their homes.

Gardening was not my only enjoyment. I also liked to build things. This is apparently a gene that runs through my family and I was just beginning to test it out. Johannes' birthday was coming up and it was never easy to get him a gift. That year I had a great idea. Every time we went to Bangkok we would stop at a small road-side restaurant along the way to use the restroom. (No this is not another latrine story.) As you would walk around the building to the back, there was a large cage of parakeets which would always amuse us. So it was my idea to build a bird cage which we would put down in our lanai. Now the only tools I had were a hand saw, a screw driver and a hammer, but I was undeterred. I went down to the local lumber store and bought my wood supplies. Then with my design in mind of an old Thai house, I began to work out under our carport. Each day as I finished working I would have to haul all the pieces to hide them behind the maid's quarters so that when Johannes came home he would not see what I was doing.

It took me three weeks to construct this thing that was seven feet high, five feet wide and about three feet deep. Finally it was such a huge piece that I could no longer move it, so even though it was not quite the day of his birthday, I decided to give him his present. He had slept in that Sunday and when he awoke, I said come see what I was giving him for his birthday. He came down to the kitchen door and looked out to the carport. Now this carport was a good 100 feet from the door and the cage was laying on its side, but Johannes took one look and said, "Oh, a birdcage!" I could only think that someone had told my secret to him, but he insisted that no one had clued him in. So I was left with a certainty that there had been a telepathic transfer from my mind to his. After all, I had been thinking and even dreaming "birdcage" for three weeks.

My initial occupants of the cage were two pairs of parakeets, Sam The Man, Ornery Aggie, Sweet Susie and The Professor. This was my first experience with birds and I was amazed at the different personalities they had. It didn't take too long before I had twelve birds in my cage. Hollowed out coconuts were used as nests and the first time my adults had a batch, I was very concerned about the babies falling out of the nest so I put up some cloth beneath the coconut to catch them. I did not know yet that these babies come out flying – no problem at all. What a joy it was to watch our birds, and I still have parakeets in my home.

There is yet another critter story that comes to mind when I think of that house. In Thailand there is a lizard called a "took-gae." From head to tip of tail it is about 16 inches long, colored pail blue with orange spots, and I was told it had a poisonous bite. I am sure it got its name from the sound it made which was a long drawn out "took-gae" in sets of three.

One time I was entertaining a guest who was going to spend a few days with me, and I was telling her about how the previous family who lived in the house had a daughter who occupied what was now my guest room. She had posted a sign on the door saying "Beware of the took-gae" which was living in the air conditioning housing of her room. I went on to explain in detail about this lizard, but not to worry because I had not heard him since I moved in. Wouldn't you know! That night he reappeared and my guest came screaming out of her room in stark fear, refusing to enter the room again. Even though I banged around with a hammer on the walls, she chose to sleep on a cot in my sewing room.

As a foreigner you have to almost expect that you will be a target for thieves in the area. We had made a habit of always locking our bedroom door at night, and this time it was fortunate that we did. The day before I had been very busy preparing for a Thanksgiving dinner I was giving for some guests. I had bought lots of beer, wine, had baked bread and the kitchen was well stocked with as many of the traditional trimmings as I could find in that far away place. I had cleaned the house, and for some unknown reason had changed the place of a small lacquer box, which contained all the interior keys of the house, from our bedroom to the hallway display case. In the middle of the night suddenly I sat bolt upright in my bed and shook Johannes awake. Someone was trying to unlock our bedroom door (there were four keys of like design from which he could choose). The robber must have heard me yell because all went quiet. We waited a while and then opened the door and crept out. No one was around, but at the bottom of our staircase was the large machete I used in the garden. The back door was open and I soon found that all the beer, wine and bread were gone from the refrigerator. That seemed to be the only things missing, and we were just grateful that this "kamoy" did not find the correct key on his first try.

    We also have some great memories from that house. The tradition of giving departmental parties in the garden was carried on for my husband's birthday and also a New Year's water festival called Songkran. By now I had these parties down to a system and with the help of my wonderful maid, it was no sweat. The food and drinks were mostly the same each time and there was always someone else who arranged the entertainment. Many times a group of children, all dressed in traditional Thai costumes, would perform dances, someone usually had a guitar and there were always toasts to be made. Songkran was about blessing each other with water. We would provide a huge "klong" jar with water, a little perfume and roses floating on the surface. There were special small silver (aluminum these days) bowls used to scoop out water and pour it over the folded hands of the person you wanted to bless with good luck and prosperity. For an added measure, the blessed person would also be smeared on the face with white perfumed paste. By the end of the day you would be mostly white paste from head to foot. And as the day wore on and the beer flowed, someone would always throw some ice into the water so now you would be "blessed" with ice water down your back. At some point, Johannes and I would always be set on chairs, everyone would file past with a water blessing, and then we would be presented with new shirts. But after we had changed into these, we would be thoroughly doused again. There was no getting out of it, but it was all in great fun.

Another beautiful holiday was Loy Kratong which came about in November. On this occasion you would make or purchase a "kratong" which was a piece of styrofoam adorned with flowers, usually a lotus, some coins and a candle. These would be floated out on a river or ocean with the idea that it was a prayer for all good things to come back to you. Hopefully, your kratong would not tip over and douse the candle which was an omen of bad luck. One year we celebrated Loy Kratong on a river boat in Bangkok. The problem was that it was a very swiftly moving river and was almost impossible to float the kratongs without them tipping over. I don't remember any particular bad luck resulting for myself, however.

A very memorable party was the "beef tasting party." Our company had decided to get into the business of fattening steers on pineapple waste for sale mostly to McDonalds in Bangkok. The pineapple would tenderize the meat while on hoof, supposedly. But when the first steers were ready for slaughter, it was decided to test the meat first, so a party was planned. They cut the steer in half, poured the local brew liberally over the carcass and stuck it in a refrigerator for <u>two weeks</u>. Then they brought it to my house and laid it out on my kitchen counter. At this time I had been vegetarian for a number of years, so the sight and smell was quite revolting to me. But I did my best and began to carve up this half a cow laying there all raw on my counter. This looked like rib eye steak and that looked like rump roast and on it went until I had it all in little pieces. Then I mixed up my own teriyaki marinade, covered the

Hua Hin, Thailand

meat and it was probably in my refrigerator for a few more days before the party began. I never tasted the final product, but all agreed that it was very tender and a huge success. I thought maybe all the beer they consumed had something to do with their judgment, but I could be wrong. And I must admit that McDonalds did agree to buy the product.

Large company parties were also held at our club house near the center of town. They would set up tables on the basketball court with a bandstand on one end. Everyone from the company would be invited so there would be hundreds of employees and their families. A generous buffet of foods would be provided and lots to drink.

In the afternoon there would be a game of "tak raw," which could be compared to badminton, except there was no racket, a wicker ball was used, and no hands were allowed to touch the ball. The feet and body were used, much like European football. I loved to watch this game because it was almost like a ballet. There would be three men on each side of a net about the height of a badminton net. One man at the net would toss the ball to the "server" standing outside the court like in tennis. But the server would have his back to the net, looking over his shoulder for the ball, and then leap into the air twisting and kicking the ball over his shoulder and thus over the net. The grace and athleticism was something to behold!

The band would start off pretty good, in my opinion, and then after maybe five or six songs, that would be the last of western music and what followed would be Thailand's version of popular songs. There would always be a lead female singer and it was enough to set your teeth on edge. It was about this time that I would begin to get very tired and be thinking of leaving early, but you were almost required to get up and dance at least one round of a traditional Thai dance called "ramwang" where you had to move your hands in a specific manner. I was glad that I had been a hula dancer, but it still was not enough for me ever to master that dance.

The club house was a gathering place for company people because of a swimming pool, tennis and basketball courts, a small bar lounge, a kitchen and a general meeting room with lots of tables and chairs. This was a logical place for me to begin teaching craft classes to some of the people working for the company. My friend Pom would put up a notice at the office of the next class and people would sign up. For my part, I had to be certain that the craft was mostly something to be done only with your hands because nobody could afford to buy special tools. The first class was macramé. I found a place down at the market selling fishing supplies and was able to get plenty of cords to use. From my business that I had in Davao, I had a big stack of pattern books, and I chose a plant hanger that was not too difficult but still incorporated all the basic knots. About ten people signed up and we had such a good time that the word spread and my next class had about 30 girls.

Moving on, I decided to try soft sculpture dolls. This required some preliminary sewing on a machine, but I could easily handle that and the rest was all hand work. Well, let me tell you, it was as if these girls were all 8 years old the way they got excited about their dolls. Since the final product was about the size of a new born child, they all brought baby clothing to dress their dolls and then it was a frenzy of picture taking with all the dolls lined up on a bench, all of them as cute as could be.

One of the last classes I taught was weaving. For this I only had three students, and we actually built the table looms first. Then after teaching them the basics by doing a sampler, they all did a small project. One girl who excelled made a lovely blouse, first weaving the fabric and then cutting and sewing the

Hua Hin, Thailand

final piece. She was so proud and it gave me such pleasure to have passed on one of my own passions.

Yes, weaving did become a serious passion while there in Hua Hin. Another American woman had come to live there and she had a gorgeous eight harness floor loom which I hungered to have. So I hired a carpenter who copied her loom. Then my husband's man in charge of all equipment on the plantation did all the metal work. The result was great in that now I could at last do some intricate weaving that was not possible on the loom I had built in Davao. This opened up a whole new world to me of weaving Swedish lace and other intricate designs where you needed multiple harnesses. I learned that I loved working in very fine threads for the challenge it presented. One masterpiece of weaving that I am proud of is a shawl made from some raw silk threads. It was not easy to acquire these threads, however, and the only reason I was able to do so was because the daughter of a family who ran a silk weaving business happened to work for the company, and she offered to get me a couple skeins. The silk is very, very fine and it took me months to accomplish the task of weaving this five foot long shawl, but the reward was immense.

To feed this passion for weaving, I had to find stores in Bangkok to buy my supply of threads and that meant a taxi ride to Chinatown on almost every monthly trip. This was an adventure all in itself. Besides hunting for a source of my weaving supplies, I also would go to the "Thieves Market" which had wonderful shops full of brass and antiques. You had to use all your bargaining powers to navigate that place. One day I spotted a "noodle stand" which was a brass box with glass doors about 24 inches high. There were shelves inside and small brass bowls that hung off the sides. This was used by local vendors selling noodles on the streets, but I saw it as a décor item. Anyway, I already knew a price because I stopped another woman on the street who had just bought one before I entered the shop. So I began my bargaining at about half that price. Oh, the man in the store ranted that I was taking the shirt off his back and we went back and forth, finally arriving at a price just 50 cents U.S. away from each other. I would not go up and he would not go down, so I walked out of the store. Now I really <u>did</u> want that noodle stand, but it was the principle of the thing. It took only about 30 seconds for the shop owner to come running down the street with a lower offer which I, of course, accepted. That felt so good; there is nothing so rewarding as winning.

Then there was the cloth market which had a thousand stalls under one roof selling all manner of cloth. It was crowded, dusty and primitive, but it was also a treasure hunter's paradise. Across the street was Sam Paeng Lane which was a street meant for only pedestrians, but you always had to be careful of the motorcycles and carts hauling merchandise to the vendors. It was a fascinating place with all the smells of the Orient from "pharmacies" selling powdered rhino horns to the food vendors selling curries. I loved going there and never failed to find items of interest.

Another market was one selling only religious articles. I was asked by a friend back in the United States to buy a "Ganesh" as a wedding gift to someone. I had no idea what this was, but I went down to this dark and dusty market and asked around. There were tables and tables of amulets, bronze statues and other religious items, and I was lead to this one particular statue of an elephant with many arms. It was actually a Hindu god, but since the Buddists of Thailand mixed in some Hindu rituals also, it was not surprising to find that statue here. Away I

Hua Hin, Thailand

went with my prize and a feeling that there in Bangkok you could find just about anything in the world.

And, oh my, the wonderful jewelry to be had! It was so cheap. You just had to be a bit careful to only buy from a store recommended by a trusted friend. The gold shops were everywhere, and the walls of these small stores were dripping with baht chains which were 24 karat gold. In the old days people would buy a link of gold as their means of saving money and so their wealth was worn around their neck. The weight of the gold was linked to the local baht currency. You cannot live in Thailand without buying one or several of these chains. I have been wearing my baht chain for 30 years now.

Nearing the end of our 10 year stay in Thailand, my mother became ill and I returned to Florida to care for her. I had thought I would be staying a few weeks, but that turned into six months. Finally I returned home, only to find that three days later the company was sending Johannes and I for a "look-see" trip to Santo Domingo, The Dominican Republic. This meant another journey half way around the world to just two hours away from Florida where I had just been. I have always thought that it was poor planning on the company's part to have paid all that airfare, but I am sure they did not even think of that.

We spent two weeks there before returning to Thailand to await the decision of whether the company was going to set up a new operation in that country or not. This decision did not come down for four months, and it was a time that just about drove me crazy. I could not weave because I might have to break the loom down for packing at any moment. I could not do any gardening because why spend money on plants, etc., when you would be leaving. I could not do this, I could not do that. But wait, there was one thing I could do after all. During my stay in Florida while taking care of my mother, she had asked me to carve an Eskimo doll for her which she wanted for her collection. Ya, right, Mom, like I had time to do that! But that idea popped into my mind all these months later that this was something I could do and just put it aside if we were moving. So I went down to the local lumber yard, purchased some 4x4 lumber and began carving, first the head, then two arms and legs. The body would be made of cloth. I totally immersed myself in my project and joy began to return. I even knitted a sweater for my doll and made some muck-lucks out of rabbit fur. After finishing that doll, I immediately began another of a classical Thai dancer. I went to my favorite cloth market in Bangkok and bought all the correct fabrics for her dress and even took the doll down to a local hair salon where they styled the little wig I glued to her head. The girls in the salon had a great deal of fun to do this for me and didn't even charge me a baht.

When we at last got the word that we would be leaving, it was a very sad day because we had come to love the country and its people and I knew that my life was going to be changing dramatically in our new location. Johannes left early for Holland to visit his family, and I stayed behind to pack up the house. The packers came and as they filled each box it was placed down on our lanai. I was staying at a hotel across town and when the final box was closed, it was late in the day. The truck would come in the morning. Tired, I returned to the hotel, but I got to thinking, hum, all my stuff is just sitting there, unguarded, in a screened in lanai. I am sure every "kamoy" in the area knows this and it would be simple pickings for them. So I got dressed, returned to the now empty house, found a piece of cardboard, and "slept" on the floor with my cat. I was younger then and could do that.

Our journey to Santo Domingo was about as traumatic as it gets. I was traveling again with an animal and we chose KLM

Hua Hin, Thailand

airlines because they said they had a special compartment for animals. I was going to meet Johannes at Schiphol airport in Amsterdam and I asked to be able to see my cat at that point. After the 14 hour flight I found my way to a desk to ask to see her, and, no surprise, she was lost. An airline attendant took me through the bowels of the airport looking for her carrying case. At last I saw it coming down the line with all the regular luggage (it had not been put in the special animal area on the plane) and when it finally reached us I expected to find a dead animal. I reached into the case and felt a cold body, but then she moved. We rushed to a vet on the premises and he was able to bring her back. I left her there for a few hours and went to meet Johannes and his parents for lunch before we were to board another flight to New York.

In a few hours we were on our way and I just took a sleeping pill and slept for that 9 hours. The dilemma was what to do with the cat when we had to change airlines in New York. Nobody could give us a good answer of how she would be handled, so we decided that I would get off the plane first and Johannes would handle our luggage. I would go on to the next airline (and you may know that you have to take a taxi to get from one terminal to another at La Guardia) and inquire about the cat. When I got there, I was told that the cat would be coming off with the luggage and I should go back to customs to find her. Away I raced, in a panic by this point, back to customs which by now was empty. Not a soul around. So there was nothing to do but get yet another taxi to return, and the day being what it was, the taxi dropped me off at the wrong place. I began to run because by this time the flight to Santo Domingo was probably boarding. I flew up to the counter of the Eastern Airline to ask them what gate I should go to, and they just looked at me and said, "We are closed." and they would not help me. So I turned to another counter and asked a person to just tell me what gate was written on my boarding pass because I was so flustered by this point that I couldn't figure it out. Away I ran as fast as my weary body would go and found the gate, slipped on board just as the door was closing. There was my husband and on seeing me he said, "Where the #$%^ have you been?" It's times like those that you really would rather have received a hug, no?

Thus ended our stay in Thailand, a country we had come to love for many reasons. Number one on the list were the people themselves, who would give you the shirts off their backs. We remember them as hard working, fun loving and sincere and we made friendships that will last a lifetime. Next was the exotic beauty of the countryside, from rice paddies to long stretches of deserted ocean beaches. How lucky were we to spend ten years in this wonderful place.

SANTO DOMINGO, DOMINICAN REPUBLIC
1987–1994

Santo Domingo, Dominican Republic

Our arrival in Santo Domingo that May of 1987 was like stepping into another world. It was a move I had dreaded, with leaving our beloved Thailand behind as one of the main reasons. Being one of the first three families to be moved to the Dominican Republic with the company, there was no infrastructure, no one to greet us, take us by the hand or show us the ropes. We were alone and had to figure things out by ourselves.

We were immediately faced with difficulties at every turn. There was finding a house to rent and not knowing what areas of the city were better than others. In our previous locations, we were assigned a person from the office who would gather all the information and take us around, or we would simply be assigned a house that the company already owned or rented. We didn't even think about dealing with the owner of the house or paying utilities. That was all taken care of by the office. We were coddled and protected from any hassles. But all that was changed now. It was up to us to sink or swim.

After locating a house that seemed OK for us, now we also had to find an apartment in which to live for the several months it would take for our shipment of household goods to arrive from the other side of the world. It was small but adequate, on the second floor with nice large windows to let in lots of light. No sooner had we emptied our suitcases than a hurricane hit the island with a fury. We huddled in the back bedroom and listened as the winds almost imploded those large windows. My poor cat crawled down under the covers to the foot of the bed and shook in fear. I know because I was also under those covers hiding. Fortunately, the hurricane did not make a direct hit and the city was spared severe damage.

I had been away from the Spanish language for 15 years and it was not easy for me to pick it up again. Add to that the fact that Dominicans spoke a dialect of Spanish which was very rapid and they usually cut off the last portion of words, giving you the feeling that they were speaking an entirely different language, or that they had mashed potatoes in their mouths. They also used different words for things than were used in Costa Rica, so now I had that added vocabulary.

One such word, "apagone," meaning the electricity was gone, we learned very fast because it was a daily occurrence. "Se fue la luz." You would hear all the maids in the building hollering and then there would be a big crescendo of the noise of generators being cranked up in the neighborhood. It sounded like you had a large semi truck parked in your front yard, revving its motor, and the smell of diesel filled the air. Every home had a light socket placed strategically with a bulb that would come on when the "Llego la luz" (the lights are on) signal was sounded. Peace would reign once again.

These "apagones" affected so much of life in the city. Obviously, you had your refrigerator to think about, but also, since there were no generators to fill the gap, street stoplights did not function. Here is where a personality trait of the Dominicans was laid bare. If you were driving when the lights went out, you could always know because there would be traffic tie ups like you would not believe at intersections. Everyone wanted to be first and would find whatever path, even the sidewalk, to get through. Consequently, a solid mass of cars would halt all flow and even motorcycles could be caught in the middle. I'm not kidding! At first sight of such a jam, I would try to make a U-turn to find some side street to divert to in order to make any progress. Many times I would not be lucky and the only way for the jam to be released was if some person would get out of his car and begin to untangle the mess one car at a time.

Santo Domingo, Dominican Republic

Then you also had to be aware that the refrigeration in a supermarket might be compromised so it was a game of Russian roulette to buy meat or other refrigerated items. You could always tell the ice cream which had been melted and then refrozen. You learned to open anything that could be opened to inspect it before buying, but you also realized that others were doing the same and thus compromising sanitary conditions. You just hoped you were the first to open that particular item.

There was also the problem of being able to buy gas for your car when the lights were out. Right, no electricity, no gas. It was vital that you not wait until your tank was empty before you filled it or you might be caught short.

Finally our day came for the arrival of our household goods. This was another adventure that only those who have lived abroad can imagine. Everything has to clear customs before it enters the country, and whereas in other company divisions with long histories of presence there, they knew the ropes of which official to bribe and grease the system. We did not have that knowledge yet in this division, so we were the learning curve for future families. We had to go down to the wharf to an area where they placed all the huge shipping containers and an official from the customs office came out to open and inspect inside every box. This meant taking each box out and placing it in the dirt as it was opened. One of my worries at that time was that the areas between containers were also roads that large trucks were moving along and could easily have run over one of my boxes. Finally the box containing our collection of liquor was opened (it is always illegal to ship booze) and we just told the man to take whatever he wanted. It was surprising that he only took two bottles of whiskey. It was a very long hot and dusty day, but the approval came and the next step was to load everything on our own truck for transfer to our new home.

At last we were going to get back to some semblance of a normal life. I would have all my equipment for my hobbies and life would get easier. Such is always the hope. But there were still some hurdles to jump in the process of getting settled.

The first was getting connected to the power grid of the city – what there was of it. You made an appointment for someone from the power company to come to your home to do "an estimate" of the amount of power you would use. First he counted the number of air conditioners you had and he assumed that you would be running all of them 24/7. There was no arguing that you only ran each one for a maximum of 8 hours per day. Then he counted the number of small appliances such as coffee makers, toasters, vacuum cleaners, and such. Again the assumption was of use 24/7. I think he also looked into the color of my eyes and finding them blue, the price doubled. All of this seemed unnecessary because there was a meter on the house, but what we learned was that there were no personnel to go around and read the meters. So the estimate was made. There was simply no arguing with the figure, you paid it or they would cut your lights. The frustrating thing also was that there was so little electricity anyway – we experienced brown-outs probably 14 hours a day, 7 days a week. I can, however, look on the bright side of it all and believe that this was a wonderful lesson in appreciation of all the things one takes for granted in our great United States.

A related obstacle that I learned to maneuver around was water supply. My house had a large cistern beneath the carport, and although city water was supposed to come into the house, there was not enough pressure for that to happen. So I had to rely on trucking water into the house from tanker trucks hired whenever you needed them. But, you guessed it, no electricity, no power to pump the water into the trucks, and at the end of the line, no water for me. Every morning I would go out to the cistern and dip a long pole into the tank to determine if I could do the laundry that day and still have water for Johannes to take a bath. I could never let the level get too low before calling the truck which may or may not be able to come.

I had found myself a good girl, Gisella, to work for me and she was able to show me how to do many things. This was in spite of the language barrier where she would have to repeat everything at least three times before I understood. But we laughed about that. One day I asked her the location of the open vegetable market. I had shopped in the supermarkets, which appeared modern enough, but the vegetables all looked half dead. Since my mode of operation had always been to buy at an open market, Gisella took me to the main one in town. First off, I had to drive through the slums of Santo Domingo to get there, which was a bit scary, and once there I had to literally climb over a mountain of garbage to get inside the market. The reason the garbage was there is that small push carts would buy their vegetable wares and then before venturing out onto the streets, they would peel away the outer leaves to make things look nice. No attempt had ever been made, it appeared, to clean up outside the market. Once inside I found only very local kinds of produce and I decided that it was a trip I never had to make again.

I am telling all my tales of frustration so that later I can get to the good part, which did eventually poke its head in the door. So bear with me.

The bureaucracy of this country was amazing, but it could be that it was the same in other third world countries, but we as company personnel did not have to deal with it. In Santo Domingo we did. To get a driver's license was something that previously was just a matter of signing a paper that someone brought to the house and a few days later you would magically receive your official license. Nothing like that was possible for us, however, and we had to blindly find our way through a maze of hot, dirty, smelly, local offices. The first line I got into must have had 50 people before me. There were wooden benches provided outside that you would move up one position in a process that took hours. Once inside, I was given a time and day to take my written exam. In the next line where I endured the same "musical chairs," a photo was taken. When my exam day arrived I sat again on a bench outside the room waiting for my name to be called. Finally standing at the door of the room, a guard there took my papers and then something weird happened. He shouted over a low wall to a person sitting there, "This is her first time." I noted the strangeness of that comment, but was very intent on getting into the room to take my exam. I was able to take the exam in English, which was a relief, but there was one question that I pondered and kept going back to it, so I pretty much had the question and my answer memorized. On finishing I took it up to the front for the results. This same person at the table near the entrance was to "correct" my exam, but he was also talking to another official in the room. He hardly looked at my paper but proceeded to make check marks on almost every question. Then I saw him make a check on the question I had pondered. My result was that I had failed the exam. I asked to see my exam so that I could determine which questions I had answered incorrectly, but the official refused and tore up the paper. I was upset, but could do nothing. After returning home, I looked up the question I had pondered and which was marked incorrect and found that I had indeed answered it correctly. Then it dawned on me – there was no way I was going to pass that exam because "It was my first time." I had not greased any palms and was paying the price.

Santo Domingo, Dominican Republic

The constant shortage of basic supplies could, at times, bring you to your knees. The word would go out on the magic grape vine and you better drop everything and get yourself down to the supermarket because the supply of toilet paper (or maybe sugar or flour, sometimes chicken) was dwindling. A long line of people would snake through the isles and each cart was allowed one bag of whatever. One Christmas season there was no sugar or flour so there were no special holiday goodies that year.

One year there was a major gas shortage and this created a whole new occupation in the country – car pushers. The first rule was to NEVER let your car get below half full. The second rule was to get in line early because it was going to take hours to get to the pump. In the meantime you could turn off the ignition and a "car pusher" would advance your car in line. You could even go sit in a nearby restaurant while waiting. And the apagones could also prolong the wait because electricity was used to pump the gas from the underground tanks. It all came down to patience, and I got very good at that.

I am about finished now with griping about all the bad stuff of living in Santo Domingo. It is not in my nature to dwell too long on such things but much prefer to turn my attention to happier endeavors.

This was a large international city with embassies from all over the world, so at any gathering many countries would be represented. I think the second day after my arrival I was invited to a sewing tea which was held every Tuesday in someone's home. Everyone would bring some hand work to do, but mostly it was a place to exchange ideas and stories. And, of course, drink coffee, tea and eat lots of sweets. Every hostess tried to outdo the other.

From this tea party I learned of a mahjong group which I was very keen to join. They also met once a week and there would be three or four tables of women. This was not the mahjong that I knew, however, since we had women from Germany who played German mahjong, Filipinas who played their version and Americans who had a very different set of rules, and so on. Since one German woman seemed to have a control issue, most tables were trying their best to play her version, but I noticed right away that she would conveniently remember some new rule when it benefited her. I brought this subject up with several of the women and we decided to make a Dominican mahjong set of rules. We would take a few of the rules from here and some from there and print them out for all to study and we could all be on the same page. The German woman, needless to say, was not too pleased with our new version, but the group as a whole was happier.

Then there seemed to be a steady barrage of parties to attend and also to host. Many men higher up in the company were coming to see how this new division was being set up and we three families took turns to host dinners for them. Later we were relieved of this "duty" when the company chose a nice restaurant in the area where we could have a private room.

With all these activities, my life had taken a 180 degree turn from the isolation of Hua Hin to this frenzy of social activities. At times I felt frustrated and infringed upon when I could not find time for my hobbies. I had to learn to say no.

Another thing that changed our lives was the availability of receiving television broadcasts from the U.S. We were immediately addicted and our evenings were no longer about reading books. It had been twenty years since we had a TV and this was a whole new world right in our own home. I even enjoyed watching commercials!

Santo Domingo, Dominican Republic

About six months after arriving in Santo Domingo, I met a new woman who had come to the sewing tea. During that tea we planned a bus tour of the company's pineapple plantation. While riding along this new lady, Carole, made an announcement that she would be starting oil painting classes. I immediately signed up. Although I did have some painting experience, I had never had any classes and this was something right down my alley, and I just knew I would love it.

This was the beginning of our friendship which is now in year 23. We became like sisters. I spent three years in her classes, and during that time we would often go on "photo shoots." The two of us would pack our cameras, get in our car and drive out of town looking for interesting things to photograph. Usually we wanted to find local people in their homes or perhaps pretty seascapes. On one trip, we found a small village where the homes were tiny rough board shacks. Those in better condition would perhaps have a tin roof, but many had a thatch made of palm fronds. The villagers were always very excited to greet us and have their pictures taken, offering us a chair and something to drink. The children crowded around and were happy to receive the candy we always brought. One old man was so photogenic that we asked to take his picture in his home. He lead us down a path to this tiny house with its dirt floor and he sat down in a rocker to pose for us. The lighting was perfect with the sun shining on him through the door. He was thrilled to be so important, and we were rewarded with wonderful shots of this wrinkled old man in his rocking chair. From this reference I painted a picture which sold almost immediately.

In another village along the road we stopped and were soon surrounded by people. The houses were so colorful with bougainvillea bushes adding splashes of red against the turquoise paint on the walls. As we were taking our pictures, this large group of people gathered, wanting to be in the picture. No problem, we just kept shooting. Later on looking closely at the prints, we saw that one of the villagers was actually holding the head of a cow! There is no understanding why anyone would want to do that.

Every spare moment was spent up in my studio painting. Sometimes I would have three or four paintings in progress at the same time, two which I would work on during class and then one or two that I would work on by myself. There was a never ending supply of inspiration, what with all the interesting landscapes, seascapes, and market people. At times I would get my maid to pose for me, maybe holding a pot or flower. I didn't ask her to pose nude, but would usually paint a nude figure, working from the photograph.

At some point I was introduced to a new craft from another company wife who was taking a class in stained glass. It immediately appealed to Carole and me, and we signed up for the beginner's class. Although we had a difficult time to understand the instructor's Spanish, we were smitten and I could now write a whole book about our adventures with working with glass. After our first class, in which we learned the basics, we furthered our education by asking many questions at glass stores and learning on our feet. My love of working with glass endures to this day and has given me countless hours of joy. Come to my house and see my treasures.

My maid, Gisela, would go to her own village on weekends where she had a boyfriend. One thing lead to another, and I soon learned that she was pregnant with her second child. I was fine with this and knew we could work around it. She was a good girl, needed the money, and I didn't want to fire her, so I began to sew some maternity outfits for her to wear during her

Santo Domingo, Dominican Republic

pregnancy. As her time approached, she made arrangements for her hospital stay and then we decided that we needed a trial run for me to drive her to the hospital. We enlisted the help of her brother who had a motorcycle and I was going to follow him through those unfamiliar streets down in the poor section of the city. But that day his cycle broke down and he did not show up. And, as any pessimist would expect, Gisela went into labor that night. She waited until morning to tell me which meant that she was already having pains fairly close together when we started off in the car. I was saying prayers to any God that would listen that she did not have that baby on the floor of my car! And here I was heading into a part of the city I did not know. I had to stop every short while to ask directions, but we finally arrived. There were several other expectant mothers in the waiting room, and no nurses or doctors in sight. I ran down a hall to try to locate ANYONE to help. A very unconcerned nurse humored me and came out to the waiting room to see what this frenzied foreign woman was yelling about. By this time Gisela was sitting on the floor and it was obvious the event was about to take place. They found her a bed and handed me a list of medicines and syringes that I had to go out and buy at a local pharmacy because the hospital had nothing. I kid you not! Since there was nothing else for me to do after accomplishing that, I went on home to wait a few hours before returning. Later that day I found her in a room filled with other mothers. Gisela was laying on a bed with no sheets and her new born son was at her side on this bare mattress. It was hot, smelly and primitive, but I guess if you survive this kind of entry into the world, you can survive many things.

Gisela and her infant son Paul lived with us another couple years before she decided to return to her village to get married. I bid her farewell and began the search for a new maid. This is how I came to find Eladia, the <u>Best Maid on the Planet</u>

Earth. She had a wonderful sense of humor, a non-stop work ethic, and the heart of a saint. One day I found her in her room crying with her television on and I enquired what was the matter and she told me that she had just seen a news program of some natural disaster on the other side of the world where many people had died and she was crying for them. The poor woman also had a list of phobias which must have been difficult to deal with when you live so "close to the earth" as she had her whole life. One was a fear of frogs. Her belief was that if a frog pees in your eye, you will go blind. Now I ask you, what are the chances of that? But it was real to her. Now and again I would hear this blood curdling scream and I would have to hurry to the rescue. It was usually a tiny, one inch tree frog that had found its way into the house.

Not long after Eladia began to work for us, I received notice that the owner of our house was going to sell it. I was happy about this because the neighborhood had become very noisy and I wanted to get away from such a busy street. My husband, however, had other thoughts and firmly put his foot down saying, "We are not moving until the house is sold, punto." He always followed the path of not causing undue expenditures for the company and this move to him just might not be necessary if the house did not sell. So that was the beginning of my tale of "How I took matters into my own hands." It came to pass that Johannes had to leave on an extended business trip and would not be home for about one month. He had no sooner left for the airport than I received a call from the owner that the house had been sold. I took this as legitimate reason to find a new house immediately. It just so happened that my friend Carole had been out walking in a neighborhood she had just recently moved into near the botanical gardens, and she met a neighbor who was going to put his house on the market for rent. Carole quickly called me, I

Santo Domingo, Dominican Republic

hopped in my car to look at the home and found it to be lovely. Done deal. I called the office to schedule a truck to move my furniture, and Eladia and I went over to get everything clean and ready for our move the next week. By the time Johannes returned, we were all settled into this new house high on a hill overlooking the gardens across the street.

When the company driver picked him up at the airport and began to drive to the new house, Johannes couldn't understand why the driver was taking such a different route home. This befuddled husband came in the front door and could hardly believe what had happened. But I had a strong argument, don't you think. After all, the old house had been sold, so what else could I do? Sometimes not asking your husband first is the only way to fly.

This new house had a unique feature that I so enjoyed. The whole house was built around a central planter that was about ten feet square. The second floor was open to this planter below and had plants all around the opening which cascaded down to the first floor. There was a large sky light in the roof over it all so the house was flooded with wonderful light. I had a great time "landscaping" this planter and used the same log I had found on the beach in the Philippines so many years ago as a focal point with a few orchids attached to it.

The whole house had marble floor tiles which were cool to the touch. These were my salvation during this time of my life as I began coping with "the big M" (menopause). My symptoms manifested as night sweats where I would wake up in a pool of sweat, roll out of bed and lay my body down on those cool marble tiles. I clearly remember that feeling of relief, that is until the tiles would begin to heat up. That's when I would take a quick shower, grab some towels which were always ready for laying down on the wet bed, and try to get a few more minutes of sleep. I would go through this scenario several times every night, and how I managed to function during the day is a total mystery. Somehow a woman gets through it and she is stronger because of it.

I feel I must give you another snake story, I had so many over the years. This one I can only relate through the eyes of my friend Carole. My maid Eladia had another phobia which I am sure many could relate to and that was a fear of snakes. By this time I had long since laid my own fear of that critter to rest. Here is the lead up to my story. One day I was in my kitchen and opened the silverware drawer. Draped across the drawer I found the shed skin of what appeared to be a very large snake. Of course, I checked to see if the snake was still attached, remembering my other story in Thailand, but he had finished his peel, and no amount of pounding on the floor of the cabinets could disclose where the owner of that skin could be. In the Third World, you sort of take for granted that construction of houses is going to be somewhat inferior to our great United States, so I looked around for the hole to the outside and found a small opening around the gas line which hooked up to our propane tanks outside. I tried to plug it up and hoped for the best. About one week later, again opening the same drawer, this time the REAL snake was inside and he was HUGE and black. He beat a fast retreat out the back of the drawer and down into the cabinet. I once again used a hammer to bang around on the floor boards, could not find him, and assumed there was still a hole I had not blocked up. Not knowing if the snake was still in the house, it was a quandary if I should fill up any holes or not.

Another week passed and Johannes and I went out to some company function. Late at night when we returned I found that all my blue and white ceramic collection of pots and plates had been moved from the display case onto the dinning room

Santo Domingo, Dominican Republic

table. WHAT? Eladia was still awake and here's her story, which I will piece together also from what Carole told me. Carole, who lived only one block away, received a frantic telephone call from Eladia. She was screaming, "Senora, Senora, Come Quickly!" Carole flew to the rescue and was presented with the tricky situation of a large black snake coiled up behind a plate on the display shelves. She asked Eladia, who was still screaming and almost incapable of functioning at this point, to find a broom and a pillowcase. Meantime, one by one, Carole carefully removed all the ceramics from the shelf, until there was only the last plate left in front of the snake. As she gingerly took that last piece away, the snake remained coiled, but at the moment that she brought the broom up to jam it down on the head, the snake lunged at her, fortunately missing. But this left the snake's head vulnerable and Carole plunged the broom down onto its neck and grabbed the back of the head with her other hand. What a trooper! She had Eladia holding the pillowcase open and she wrestled the snake into it and tied it shut. At this point Eladia felt a bit braver and began to beat the pillowcase mercilessly with the broom. Later, in the light of day, I killed the thing which was still wiggling in the pillowcase. According to Eladia, it was necessary to cut the head off and bury it in a different place than the rest of the body so that the mate could not come around and find you.

Another rather frightening experience happened in that house with a "snake of a different color." On a quiet Sunday morning, Johannes had gone off to the office, as was his habit, for a few hours and I was taking a shower when I heard the bell on our gate ringing. I figured it was some kids in the neighborhood going around ringing doorbells and I did not respond. Again the bell rang and again I did not respond. After a short while I had gotten dressed and was descending the stairs when I heard a very loud "kaboong" sound of metal on metal coming from the kitchen. I raced in there to see a metal bar being used to pop off my window bars. Several bars were already removed and only a couple remained before the robber had easy entry. I began to yell for help to my husband as if he were in the house, and this was enough to alert the neighbor's security guard who climbed up a ladder against the wall between our houses and began to wave his gun at the robber, who wisely ran off. It seems that the guy had first tested the house to see if anyone was home by ringing the bell several times. If no answer, probably he was thinking he was home free. I made a small donation to the neighbor's guard and hopefully the word went out not to mess with the foreigners on the hill.

For many years now, I had been a vegetarian and subscribed to a vegetarian magazine. One day Carole came to me asking if there were any spas advertised in that magazine because she wanted to take a couple weeks off. I was sure I had seen many advertised, but when I began to search, I could only find three listed. Two were in the northeast of the United States and one was only about two hours away near Miami. So that was her choice. I got to thinking about it and thought that I too wanted to go. So we packed our bags and headed off for a two week stay at this spa, not really realizing what we were getting ourselves into. It turned out that the spa was "vegan" meaning no animal products, like milk or cheese, eggs. Also coffee was off the list. Do you know that you even have withdrawal symptoms from <u>decaffeinated</u> coffee?

Our first day there we read the list of activities on the daily schedule and thought that we were required to participate in each and every event. It started with an early morning meditation on the beach, followed by a run on the boardwalk. Then we had breakfast which consisted of a large plate of watermelon. From there we attended a lecture on nutrition given

Santo Domingo, Dominican Republic

by the doctor at the spa, followed by a class in water aerobics. There was just time to change into something to wear to lunch, which was always an interesting vegan dish. I think we may have had an hour to rest before we headed for the gym to use some machines. Then another lecture before the evening meal. At about 7pm there would be a guest speaker which you surely could not miss. By 9pm you would race back to your room to don your still damp swimsuit for a casual jacuzzi session to discuss the day's events.

After two days of this, our shared room looked like a disaster area, like one of Florida's notorious hurricanes had swept through. There were clothes everywhere and wet towels lay wadded in corners for lack of a place to hang them. We took a minute to look around and realized other more experienced guests were picking and choosing the events they wanted to do. We could step off from this frantic pace and still get good results. We started to schedule facials or massages and began to destress which was, of course, the reason we were there.

Over the next five years, we went to that spa about three more times, but we learned to rent a car so that we could get some shopping in during our stay. One year we hit every Goodwill store in the area – the car was on automatic and would just turn into a parking lot all by itself. Our aim was to buy lamp bases for our new hobby of stained glass. That year we took home 13 lamps, all taken apart and tucked into every empty nook in our suitcases. Yes, they weighed a ton, but it was well worth the effort.

We both took the step of dropping animal products from our diet, taking to heart all the things we had learned in the nutrition classes at the spa. But I decided to take yet another direction when I began to read about the Ann Wigmore Institute in Puerto Rico. This school taught the "Living Food Lifestyle" and I decided to attend a two week class at the institute. I was housed in a dormitory along with about 5–6 others from various parts of the world. One couple came all the way from Greece. We were taught to grow all our own food, harvest and prepare it. The early morning class was taught around a picnic table while we cleaned the various types of sprouts that we would consume later. Everything was eaten raw with the idea that cooking kills the enzymes. Every day we would cut and juice some wheat grass, which was difficult for me to swallow. It is sweet on your tongue as it first enters your mouth, but as the liquid moves to the back of your throat, there is a bitterness that is literally hard to swallow. The list of therapeutic benefits from wheat grass fills a whole page and I will always turn to it if, dread the thought, I should ever contract a life-threatening disease.

My two weeks at the institute were broken up by a weekend trip across the island to San Juan, the capitol city. The Greek couple, Katarina and Ioannis, and I rented a car to make the drive. Before we had put the car in drive, however, they required a long prayer spoken in Greek, I guess for our safety. This was OK with me. I didn't mind covering all the bases. So off we went and enjoyed all the scenes along the way.

We took turns driving and I found myself in the driver's seat on our way home when a rain storm suddenly came up, so intense that it was difficult to see the side of the road. In my experience, since there was no real shoulder to the road, it was better to just keep progressing slowly rather than pulling over to stop because you risk being rear ended. But in the minds of the other two, apparently they were petrified with fear and were screaming for me to stop the car. I did not stop, however, since I called the shots being in the driver's seat. And I just kept

Santo Domingo, Dominican Republic

thinking, hey, you guys spent ten minutes praying to God for our safety. Don't you trust him to do that?

I spent the next year diligently sticking with the program of Living Food Lifestyle. My maid, who fried the life out of all her food, thought I was CRAZY. But I grew my sprouts and fermented my rejuvelac from wheat berries and ate everything raw. I must say I have never felt better in my life. I was never sick, was very slim and had wonderful energy. BUT, the thing that tipped me off the wagon was travel. Every time I went away on a trip, my crops would die and have to be restarted upon my return, which meant a couple weeks to get back in the saddle. It got to be just too much work, so I decided to return to my vegan ways, and I would keep the Living Food Lifestyle as an "ace in my pocket" if I ever needed it.

Since living in Thailand I had found this love of keeping parakeets. I had dismantled the large cage and had it shipped along with all my household goods when coming to The Dominican Republic. In reconstructing it, things were never quite the same, but it still functioned and I placed it on my front porch and filled it with two pairs of birds. One day I looked out to my front yard and saw a little blue parakeet on the sidewalk. At first I thought one of my own had escaped, but a quick count ruled that out. Apparently someone else's pet had gotten out. Soon this young bird found my cage and began clinging to the outside as if desperate to get inside. I tried to coax him into a small cage with some food, but he was not buying that. So I waited until dark when I knew he could not see well, and then I just quietly crept up behind him, grabbed him and popped him inside the cage. He was home.

I had always wanted to have a canary too and decided the time had come for this addition to the menagerie. I put the cage up in my studio away from the parakeets who might interfere with his song. All was well and I was really enjoying the long repertoire of songs he would sing. But gradually he began to sing less and less. I inquired at many pet stores selling birds of just why he was losing his song and got a variety of answers, from he needs a mate, to he won't sing if he has a mate, to adding carrots to his diet, and on and on. I even recorded the few times he would sing and played it back to him, thinking to inspire him, but nothing seemed to work. Then one day I began to notice that he was doing something a bit strange. He was moving all his shredded carrots from one bin to another. In another day I saw the reason why; he had built himself a nest and had deposited an egg in the middle. AHA, he was a <u>she, and female canaries don't sing.</u> I packed him (her) up and returned to the store. The woman said she had been breeding canaries for 15 years and had only once before seen this happen. I went home with a new bird, but I had no luck with him either. He became sick and died in a few months, after which I decided not to try again because they just seemed too delicate.

It was during our stay in Santo Domingo that I had the opportunity to join the manager's wife and her kids on a trip back to Honduras where they had previously lived. They were co-owners of a small island off the northern coast, really just a sand bar large enough to build a cottage and have a few palm trees. The plan was to spend a week on the island and "hang out." The journey to arrive there was very involved. First we had to fly via Miami to Tegusegalpa, the capitol city. From there a smaller plane took us down to La Ceiba on the coast. A still smaller flight brought us to another island that was large enough for a landing strip. From there we had to go by a small motor boat. All supplies had to be brought in by this same small boat and there was a ham radio for communication with the outside world. And we were indeed far removed from anyone. But what an adventure!

Santo Domingo, Dominican Republic

We were a group of about 10 people and there were various types of beds available. I slept in a small structure to the side of the main house big enough for one bunk bed. Others had beds that were sofas during the day. Still others just opted to sleep in hammocks slung under the main house or between two palms. It was a casual arrangement to say the least. Fresh water was precious so bathing was not insisted upon. There was, however, one of those sun heated bags of water that you could stand under if the stickiness got too bad.

I was amazed at the organizational skills of the hostess. Everyone had different schedules of comings and goings that she kept straight in her mind, never writing anything down. She had to call on the radio for the boat to come pick up this person and drop off those supplies and in general kept the place running smoothly. There was ample supply of food and drinking water which all had to be brought in by boat.

Our days were spent mostly in the water snorkeling around the island. That was so very exciting. The routine was to suit up right after breakfast and spend the next 3–4 hours swimming around the coral reefs that surrounded the island. I had bought one of those throw away under water cameras specially for this trip, but when I took it out in the water with me, the waves were battering me around and I thought there was no way I would get a clear picture from the whole roll. But I went ahead and tried anyway. There were beautiful huge purple fan corals that nestled among white brain corals and many other types. All manner of fish abounded and the rainbow colored parrot fish were especially lovely. I saw flounders, many angel fish, puffer fish and even saw barracuda. I did my best to stay out of their path, however. At times I would look around and find that I had wandered away from the other swimmers, and that was worrisome, but then I would see a snorkel up ahead and feel reassured. Swimming out in the ocean like that was not easy going and after several hours I would return exhausted to shore.

Lunch would be waiting for us prepared by a couple maids brought along to do anything that smacked of work. It would be all I could do to eat before finding an empty hammock to take a nap. Ah, life on a remote island was not all that bad.

One day the plan was to travel by boat to another small island to hunt for shells. Away we sped, crashing over the waves which sent sprays of salt water over us until we were thoroughly drenched and sticky. But that day produced one of my most precious memories in my life. As we were speeding along, suddenly a pod of dolphins came to "play" with us. They surrounded the boat and raced along beside us. At times they would leap into the air doing one of their fantastic spins and flips, all for our entertainment. It absolutely took my breath away. I was screaming, laughing and crying all at the same time. And it all was over in a matter of moments as they swam away, bent on their own agenda. I bring that memory out at least once a year to relive those moments of sheer joy.

All too soon the week was over and it was time to retrace my steps to go home. It began with that boat ride, but there were some catches. First off, a storm had come up so the waves were absolutely huge. We huddled under tarps to try to keep dry, but that really didn't work. When we arrived at the island where we were to meet the small plane, I had to find some area to change my clothes. There was no terminal building, but on the dock where we tied up the boat, there was a small counter which I ducked down behind and stripped almost naked. It wasn't easy being curled up in a ball, very wet and sticky with salt spray and trying to pull on dry clothes. The alternative was to just get on that plane as is, which I was not willing to do. To add to the drama, the nearby plane already had its engines turning, so I had

Santo Domingo, Dominican Republic

to work as fast as possible. I was young and could handle the situation. I wonder what my choice would be now?

Other trips were taken around our island of Hispanola. Usually we had visitors and we would make a weekend trip to entertain them. One year my dad came down from Florida and we went whale watching on the north side, about a four hour drive away. My friend Carole went along, as I remember. The whales would come at that time of year to spawn. We booked a tour on a boat with perhaps 20 other people and headed off to sea. A spotter would tell us all to look off in one direction or another, and we would see the back of a whale as it swam along, a gentle appearance and disappearance of its back and occasionally we would see the tail. All the pictures I took that day showed nothing but a tiny gray spot in a vast ocean of water. Not very remarkable at all, so I still had whale watching on my "bucket list."

It was on another trip to Puerto Plata with Johannes' brother Tony and wife Riet that we had a very scary adventure. After staying at a nice hotel in the city, we heard about a beautiful waterfall down the road and decided to investigate. We traveled along the ocean for a good distance before cutting inland. Every now and then we would stop to get directions and finally ended up in a small village where the waterfall was supposedly close by, just on the other side of the bridge, as a matter of fact. But, the bridge had been washed out, so we were told to go off down a small road and stop at a house at the top of a hill where someone would lead us on foot to the waterfall. Adventurers that we were, away we went. Having come this far, we were not going to be stopped merely by a bridge being washed out.

We left our new four wheel drive car with all our luggage inside on the road and found our guides, who were a whole family of people, including children. Yes, they would take us to the waterfall. So off we went down a path at the back of their house. Each of us appeared to be assigned a person who walked by our side. I happened to have two young girls who chattered away in Spanish the whole time. The path got steeper and soon we were crawling over rocks and fallen trees and there was lots of mud and even a small creek to ford. I was falling behind the others, but my little girls stayed with me. Suddenly I became aware of what they were saying, and it wasn't good! I think they did not know that I understood Spanish, so they were talking with abandon, and what they were saying was, "I wonder when we are going to rob them?" I halted in my tracks and began to scream to the others up ahead that they turn around immediately. I was sure our "guides" only spoke Spanish, so they probably were in a quandary as to what I was saying in English. Johannes was reluctant, but I guess he heard the urgency in my voice and came back to listen to what I had heard. It was then that we assessed just what we had gotten ourselves into. It was not unheard of that tourists would vanish and be found dead in remote areas. Here we were going deeper and deeper into this wooded area, just to see a waterfall, leaving all our possessions neatly in the car, to which the robbers would have the key. How dumb were we anyway? I think we were very fortunate to have been allowed to retrace our steps and leave the area with no attempts of foul play by anyone. Certainly we had angels watching over us that day.

In each country that I lived in and employed maids, I always tried to give them some education if they wanted that would allow them to "improve their lot in life," after we left. The three girls in Davao were all sent to school, in Thailand Boonyen learned the business of making batik, we sent Gisela to school to learn to sew and made sure she had a sewing machine, and then there was Eladia. She did not have much formal

Santo Domingo, Dominican Republic

education so her ability to read and do math was very limited. However, she certainly was clever with a needle and spent her spare time doing lots of embroidery. So I got to thinking about a lovely fabric doll made with lots of embroidered embellishments that we could market. She took to it like duck to water and soon was turning out lovely works of art which I would peddle to the women with whom I was socializing. It took no time at all before Eladia was receiving special orders. Someone wanted yellow hair and the name of their granddaughter embroidered on the skirt. But I had to worry about her ability to handle the business end of the work, like figuring out the cost of materials and being sure to set aside enough money to buy materials for the next doll. I think of her now and again these days and wonder if she was ever able to continue her doll making after we left.

We knew our days were numbered here in Santo Domingo. It had been seven years since coming and the company was having quite a few problems to continue to function in this country and make a profit. So it was not surprising when the call came for us to leave, a transfer back to Costa Rica. We were pleased to be going back to a country which we had loved, and another reason was that we had begun to cast around for a place to retire and were thinking perhaps Costa Rica might suit us. This would be an opportunity for us to test the waters, so to speak.

I was quite an expert by this time in the art of packing. First you dispatch your husband to some far off place. He left on a trip back to Holland. With him out of my hair, I could get down to business. Usually I would pack all my most delicate items myself with boxes provided by the company. Then the packers would come in to do all the furniture. The whole process would take a couple weeks. There was the cat to take care of too and a visit to the vet was required to get her papers in order to travel.

There were always things that you easily got rid of too, like small appliances which were still working but someone wanted to buy. When you arrived in your new location, you were always allowed to place an order to the States for new things which would be brought in on one of the company's ships. Many things I just gave away to the maid. Eladia was building her own home on the north side of the island and I think I furnished the entire place with furniture, dishes and linens that I no longer needed.

We left the Dominican Republic with mixed feelings. We were excited to be returning to Costa Rica to live in San Jose, but we would miss the merengue music and good friends that we had made during our stay. Such is the life of company people.

SAN JOSE, COSTA RICA
1994–1996

San Jose, Costa Rica

The year was 1994 and we were pros by this time at picking up and moving across the world. It was just a matter of being very organized, but also realizing that you would be "in the process" for six months. This included the Look-See trip to the new location where the company would give you a week or so to look around and see what you would need to bring with you. Then there was the time it would take to pack up your belongings from your present location, ship them half way around the world, get them through customs at the other end, and set up your new house.

The set up included buying (or in my case, making) new draperies for the whole house, rebuying new small appliances for the kitchen because you had sold most everything before coming, maybe ordering new furniture because you had given much of your old stuff to the maid, and in general unpacking boxes and boxes of junk that you wished you could part with and quit dragging around the world. I don't want to even think about the money it cost the company to ship some of those useless things.

There were some collections, however, that, no matter the cost, needed to come with me. Like my rock collection from Thailand. Who could part with such wonderful memories. The boxes of shells also had to be carefully wrapped and lovingly placed back on the metal shelf which I had specially made in Davao. And my 150 baskets, each with a story, too precious to discard. My blue and white ceramics, the klong jars. My biggest concern about all my treasures is that I have no children who will look after them when I am gone. I do have some nieces and nephews who might divide up the loot, and if they will read this book, they can perhaps understand and appreciate their meaning to me.

1994–1996

My cat, Cheri, was by this time 21 years old, a grand old lady by any measure. She had traveled with me, albeit always with difficulty, around the world so was a unique animal in that respect too. Our first couple months in our new location of San Jose, Costa Rica, when we lived in a small apartment/hotel were not easy for any of us, much less her, but if she just had a pillow with a blanket thrown over the top of her, she accepted whatever was thrown at her.

The weather was terrible when we arrived, rainy and cold. It was winter and I just couldn't get warm. I wore socks and sweaters all through the day and decided to grow my hair long again since the cool weather would allow that. It had been a long time since we lived in a moderate climate and would take some getting used to it.

The first thing on the agenda was to find a place to live. We decided that an apartment would be preferable to a house since Johannes would be traveling quite a bit, leaving me alone. You always needed to be aware that as a foreigner you have a large target on your back, so security was a major issue. After searching in many parts of the city, I found a place in the subdivision of Escazu that was a building with only four apartments, had underground parking and 24 hour guards. Our place would be on the second floor, but since the building was located on the side of a hill, the apartment really was on the third floor with large windows all along the south side that looked out over the entire mountain range. I could watch the sun rise in the morning to the east and track it unobstructed by any buildings to set in the west. It was especially lovely to watch a rain storm come up and travel across the valley.

There were large flocks of the green parrots that would come to roost at night in a tree nearby. They made a lot of racket, not only while in the trees but also while in flight from

San Jose, Costa Rica

one place to another. But it was always a joy to watch them because it seemed that their existence was all about having fun.

This apartment reunited me with my old nemeses, the jalousie windows. Sitting up high on a hill with an empty lot across the street, the constant wind raised every particle of dust in the area and directed it toward our apartment, where it would find its way through those windows. I wiped, dusted and cursed, but it still kept coming. Finally, in desperation, I sealed all the windows on the north side with plastic. It wasn't pretty, but it helped.

I now had a small room designated as an office, and I put in my first new computer. I had a lot of catching up to do in this area and looked forward to the challenge, but it was daunting for an old gal like me. At least now I could get on the internet and be in closer touch with my family. Some of them were also on the internet, so we could reconnect after all those years.

The master bedroom was located on the south side with all those lovely large windows and view of the valley, but I decided that this room would better serve as my studio, so this is where I set up all my equipment, my loom, sewing machine and area to work on stained glass. It didn't take me long to plan my first project and get in the groove of life. I knew many things would be different, as they always are when you change to a new location, but the basics are the same.

One of the first things to do was to find a source of fabrics to sew new curtains and this meant a trip to the central market in downtown San Jose. I remembered the old days from our first stay in Costa Rica, and when I entered the market anew, nothing much had changed in twenty years. It was still a crowded covered building with a thousand stalls inside selling all manner of things. There was the stall selling dried spices which always smelled wonderful, the place to buy some leather goods, from belts to "bolsas" (pocketbooks), fresh produce places that spilled out onto the streets outside, kitchen ware, brooms, and on and on. You could spend hours browsing. In amongst everything were small shops selling food and if you were lucky you could find a stool to sit on while you ate.

The fabric stores along Avenida Central were many and large. This was a reflection of how life was lived in this country (and many Third World countries). You would have a seamstress to make most of your clothing so there needed to be huge stores with several floors of fabrics. This was heaven to me and once lured inside by the display windows at the front, I could spend hours and hours looking and feeling the fabrics. They all spoke to me, this one looked like it should be a jacket or here is a fabric for curtains or pants or whatever. So many ideas swirling around in my head.

You had to go to a different store to buy the notions needed to sew, like thread, lace or ribbon. These would all be tiny places and I always wondered why a large fabric store would not find some small area to also sell thread. It was not the tradition, I guess.

The narrow streets of downtown had become a nightmare to navigate, what with the new generation of Costa Ricans all seeming to own cars now. There was never a good time and you just had to take it as part of your day that you would be sitting for long periods of time at stop lights. It was best to try to avoid any streets that were near the central market because large trucks would be parked alongside, reducing the street to one lane.

Parking along the street was nonexistent and you needed to find a lot for that purpose. An attendant would take the keys and give you a ticket. One day I drove downtown with a company car which I had just received that morning. I pulled

San Jose, Costa Rica

into a lot and handed over the keys, got my ticket, and headed on foot to the stores. Later on returning to pick up my car, the attendant drove up with this silver car and gave me the keys. The first thing I noticed as I got in was that he had changed the radio station, not unusual, but then I looked around and couldn't find where to turn on the lights. I thought at first that I was just not accustomed to this new car, but then I realized that it was not my car. Actually it was a much fancier car, a BMW. I could have easily driven off with it, but "Honest Carol" came through in that moment and pointed out the mistake. I guess they were surprised but thankful for my honesty.

Walking on the downtown streets was also a bit tricky. You needed to be very "street wise," especially as a foreigner. Costa Rica had become a new center for drugs coming out of Colombia and the crime rate had skyrocketed since our first stay in the country. Before I left my apartment I would remove every last item of jewelry from my body, wear a fanny pack, and adjusted my eyes to the back of my head. I always walked as close to the buildings as possible and watched closely any children on the streets who were expert pickpockets. Many times they traveled in packs and would be carrying a piece of cardboard to hide their intentions. Sometimes the robbers would be riding on the back of a motorcycle. As a person walked along the sidewalk close to the road, the robber would just yank a purse off a shoulder and be gone in seconds. But my many years of living in these countries had served me well and I maneuvered through the perils with no incidences.

I was beginning to reunite with some of my old friends from Pandora who were now living in San Jose. They invited me to join a group of women who would put together a bazaar every year for charity. We would meet every month in someone's home and everyone would be working on some craft project that would eventually be included in the bazaar. Sometimes a letter would be read to the group from a family requesting help and these letters would be saved to be part of the pool from which we would choose once a year those that needed our help the most.

After a few months of living in San Jose, I was invited to a birthday party that changed my life. Everybody had brought a small gift, and one in particular piqued my interest. A woman from Holland had "wrapped" her gift in a small, five sided box that was itself made by her. I asked if she would be willing to loan me the directions for making this box, and this was the beginning of what could only be labeled an obsession. It was called a Victorian Sewing Box and was made from a sturdy cardboard covered with fabric, lace and ribbon. First I had to figure out the directions for making the box, and, as written, they didn't make too much sense. Then I had to begin to feel my way around making the box my own way, and as I did this, I rewrote the directions, drawing sketches along the sides to better explain the process.

It was just before a trip back to the States to visit some family that I decided to make everyone a box and ended up making 12 of them. I thought it would be great to put some in the bazaar too, so I brought one over to the president of our ladies club and she about went ape with delight. She asked that I make at least one dozen. When it was time to begin the box making adventure, I hit the fabric stores with a whole new set of eyes. Bolts of fabric would leap into my hands screaming <u>Victorian Sewing Box.</u> One was more gorgeous than the next and the mere juxtaposition of two colors would send me off on a whole new tangent of ideas. It was all very exciting and soon I had a dozen boxes in a pretty row ready for the bazaar. They never, however, reached the general public because all the women in the club bought up those boxes before they hit the floor. But money is money and makes no difference from where it comes.

Soon I had women coming to me asking that I show them how to make the boxes, and this was the beginning of craft classes in San Jose. My first class had 12 ladies. I was very organized and had all the directions carefully printed out, written in Spanish no less, for each student. I would encourage them to take notes also to be sure they understood clearly how to do it. And before class everyone would get a list of materials to buy and bring to class. It was so interesting how each student would imagine her box and choose the materials. They were all unique and every one beautiful.

After completing one box, most women wanted to make another, and since doing it in a class was so much more fun than by yourself, we had another class. I even did a second class on the other side of town for 15 more students. Some wanted to make boxes for themselves but most wanted also to contribute some to the bazaar. If I look back on all the classes I taught with this box, I can count at least 100 students over time. With each class, I had to make my own box to demonstrate the process, so you can imagine on how many boxes I have made. But I enjoyed every single one. All but one were given as gifts or sold at the bazaar so I have little to show for all of that. But how interesting to track how a simple moment in time can expand and touch so many.

During this same time I was taking my own craft class in molding leather. Calf skin was used and I found the shop down at central market where they sold the hides. It had that special smell and there were piles of hides all over the floor. You had to spread them out and check each one for flaws. One hide would cost around $20 and I could do perhaps four small projects with each. In class we would take small clay pots and stretch wet leather around them. This would dry and keep the shape of the pot, which we would remove. Then we would decorate the object with various leather pieces, perhaps flowers or braided ropes. The finished piece would be mounted on a round slice of wood.

Not long after completing the course, my "box" ladies all wanted to learn, so I began another class molding leather. It was always a challenge to find nicely shaped small pots to use, and I would frequently drive out to a neighboring village to the clay pot stores along the road to search. Some of our finished projects found their way into the bazaar, of course, as we were always looking for new things to sell.

On a visit to my sister Katy in Houston one year, I attended a sculpting class with her and became consumed with sculpting clay. I could hardly restrain myself from putting my hands on her work that day. Once back home, I asked around to find a class in San Jose and I found a small art school across town. A whole new passion took over my mind and body as I began working in this new medium. I would walk around studying people's faces, how the cheek bone lays in relation to the nose or ear. It was a new world to think "in the round" after so many years of painting on a flat surface. The first piece I did in my class was the head of a black man. I was trying to get some profound expression on his face, but whenever I looked at him, all I could think of was that he was saying, "Oh, s___!" That was not going to fly as a title for the piece, however, so I came up with the name, "illusiones quebrados" (broken dreams).

The modeling clay I was able to buy there was a very crude red clay and I had no means of going further with projects, the next step being to have your finished piece bronzed. Since that was not an option, I would just hollow out the figure and let it slowly dry. At first I would drape it in damp cloth and later just let it dry in the open. The pieces were fragile, but somehow most of them survive to this day. I learned that you could paint a faux bronze, saving myself thousands of dollars.

One day Johannes and I decided to drive out to the central valley for the day. It was a beautiful area often compared to Switzerland. Along the way we drove past a small house with a sign that it was a museum and I had to pull the car over. It wasn't the museum that caught my eye but a huge pile of wood outside that turned out to be roots of coffee trees that had been floating in the water of a nearby river. The family that owned the museum would use the roots to carve faces in them and had decorated the entire house with these pieces of art which were all for sale. The owner was surprised that I wanted to look through his pile of raw, unfinished wood, but to me each piece was already a work of natural art and I could see myself combining them with my own sculpture. He allowed me to choose several roots and just gave them to me for free. I was about in seventh heaven, not only finding these treasures, but than getting them for nothing.

My first combined sculpture was one entitled "Joy Ride." One of these coffee roots looked to me like a horse, so I sculpted a young girl riding this horse, her head thrown back and hanging on to the reigns with one hand. Another piece inspired me to mold a nude laying on the branch, dangling one hand in some imagined water below. This piece did not survive our next move so it is only a memory.

When we had left Santo Domingo, I finally had given my large flight cage with all the birds to one of the men packing our house. I knew that the cage probably would not survive another disassembly/reassembly, and we would not have room for it in our new place. I hoped the birds would adjust easily if they remained in their own cage. I missed their chatter and knew that someday I would have more birds. The day came when a company family was leaving and had to find a home for their two cockatiels. They were even giving the cage and all accessories. These were birds that were accustomed to being loose in the house with their wings clipped, so this would be a new adventure for us. My cat was so old that she would not be a danger. The birds could probably walk faster than she could. In fact, when I introduced the birds and cat in a nose to nose encounter, Cheri was so disinterested that she just lay back down on her pillow to sleep and let the birds stand right on top of her.

We hadn't had the birds too long when it was time for our annual vacation and we would be gone for about one month. I made arrangements for the neighbor's maid to come in to feed the animals, making sure that the birds stayed in their cage during this time. Since Cheri was so old, I also asked a company woman who had several pets to be a backup in case of any medical emergency.

We arrived home from vacation around 11pm and there was a message on our answering machine that I should come immediately to this woman's home. I raced over there and found Cheri laying there on a pillow. She obviously was close to death and my friend told me that she had been taking her to the vet every day for shots to keep her alive as her body had begun to shut down. She was 23 years old and that puts her well over 100 years old, human time. I carried her home and curled up with her in my arms. Then I watched her take her last breath. This cat had waited for <u>two weeks</u> for me to arrive home to say goodbye

San Jose, Costa Rica

and I will forever thank her for that gift. She had been my baby for all those years and I can't describe the pain of losing her.

But as the morning sun arose, the Saber of Death was not finished with me yet. I went in to my birds to liberate them after one month of being cooped up in their cage. I opened the door and expected them to come out and sit on my shoulders, but the female took off on her newly grown out wings, flew like an arrow across the room and slammed into one of those huge windows, and fell down dead from a broken neck.

I buried my babies together in the garden below. The gardener dug the hole and a flowering bush was planted above. I don't remember much other than the tears and pain felt for days and days, laying on the bed in a fetal position.

The original owners of the cockatiels would write now and then to inquire of their babies. I had replaced the female with one of the same color and that year I photographed them for our Christmas card. When I sent one to these people, I never told them what had happened. If they should ever read this book, I hope they can understand and forgive me.

Costa Rica had become an exotic tourist destination and my sister, Katy, her husband, John, and younger daughter, Gwen, decided to visit once again. The main attraction would be a trip to the rain forest. I booked a tour for the four of us to spend two nights at a research camp in the forest which was dedicated to the preservation of the rain forest. What a journey was to follow!

Johannes drove us to the first stop on our trek. This was a small structure on the edge of the forest. Here we unloaded our bags and I said goodbye to my husband who would return in three days to pick us up again. We were among a group of 15 people and we were all fitted with tall rubber boots. That in itself was a bit ominous, don't you think? Next we climbed up into a trailer which had wooden benches along the sides and it was pulled by a tractor. Away we went down a small dirt road and forded a shallow river before we began to climb into some foothills. So far so good. The terrain was not too difficult and the scenery spectacular.

There was an abrupt change in the path as we found ourselves heading down a "road" which became a trench. The sides of the trench were as tall as our trailer and the bottom was a quagmire of mud. Soon we were jolting over logs that had been thrown down in the mud to make the way passable. It was getting progressively harder and harder for the tractor to pull the trailer and we passengers were being thrown from side to side. It seemed better to stand and hold on rather than sit and be tossed around and bruised. Nearing the half way point, our tractor began to smoke and gave up. There was nothing to do but climb down from the trailer and head on foot to a structure about 100 yards away that was a bunk house for people who were working at the research center. It was high and dry and that was a welcome rest for us all.

From that point on there were two choices. The first was to hike through the forest on a path and about half the group chose that option. We four chose to stay with the trailer which was being hooked up to a bigger tractor. Forward we went up that trench and were told the final destination was only about two miles away. It seemed like twenty, however. Even with our much larger tractor pulling us, the journey got rougher, the road muddier and the logs fewer that were keeping us somewhat from sinking into it all. Then even the larger tractor couldn't handle it and died about one mile away from the top.

Now we had no options but to walk THROUGH THE MUD. But wait, there was yet one option and that was to laugh

San Jose, Costa Rica

at it all. And that is what we did as we began trying to put one foot ahead of the other in mud that sank us up to our hips. Now we understood the reason for the boots, but it became a real issue to pull your boot out of the mud. I was laughing so hard that I was weak and was almost unable to move forward. It took us at least one hour to reach the research station and when we did, we found the rest of the group sitting there having their lunch, looking clean and rested. We ourselves were exhausted and covered head to toe in red clay.

We got cleaned up and then enjoyed an amazingly wonderful lunch, all the ingredients of which had to come into the forest by the same route we had just taken, which made you appreciate it all the more We sat at a long picnic table under a roof and watched literally thousands of hummingbirds come to feeders all along the roof of the structure. As you looked out further into the clearing, there were many of those gorgeous large blue butterflies, almost neon in color. You would see flashes of blue light as they darted in and out of the sunshine. There was an excitement of things to come with this adventure.

That afternoon our tour guide took us down a path into the forest and we began to learn about all the different plants of the area. There was one amazing plant, a "walking palm" which could actually shift positions according to where the sun was reaching the forest floor. It would send down roots from above in the new direction and release old roots on the back side, and in tiny increments the palm would "walk" across the ground. John, my brother-in-law, is an avid photographer of insects and he was having the time of his life with all the creepy-crawly critters along the path.

I was lagging a bit behind the group when suddenly I saw an amazing sight. It was a green viper snake right on the edge of the walk which everyone else had overlooked. I yelled to the group to turn around and come see and we watched as this very poisonous snake swallowed a frog. The frog was so large that the snake was unable to move and just had to endure all the tourists snapping photographs.

That evening, after another amazing meal in the mess hall, we welcomed an early bedtime. I mean early because there in the tropics, so close to the equator, the sun goes down at about 6pm every day all year round, and in this deep forest there is not the slightest glimmer of light except the moon and stars. The station's only light was from kerosene lamps, and those were not kept burning too long because of fuel economy. So we all found our beds, and after we had freed a bat from our room, we sank into deep sleep.

The next two days passed much too fast as we enjoyed learning many things about the rain forest. Then there was the "luxurious" ride down the trench to civilization. Maybe because it was downhill, we made it all the way using only one tractor. It had been a memorable stay, and with all its difficulties, we would do it again in a minute.

There was another tourist attraction closer to the city that was a must on the list and this was a ride on an elevated cable through the canopy of the rain forest. This gave us a completely different view as we slowly moved along the line in "cars" that held 6–8 people. You could reach out and touch the branches which were dripping with bromeliads, mosses and vines. We saw large macaw birds and toucans too. There is also a type of oriole that makes a very raucous call and builds long hanging nests high in trees. I will forever think of this call when I think of a jungle setting.

When you have visitors, you try to do as many interesting things as possible and Costa Rica is a gold mine, to be sure. Most people have not seen a live volcano, so away we went to Arenal, only a two hour drive away. We reserved some rooms at the base of the volcano to spend the night, but to get to that hotel you had to ford a rather wide, swiftly moving river. We had a 4-wheel drive vehicle, but it is still a frightening thing to face crossing such an expanse when you can't see exactly where the road is or how deep it might be. My husband just gunned the motor and bullied his way across, crawling up the embankment on the other side to the relief of us all.

We settled into our hotel rooms and then drove off to the base of the volcano where there were trails you could climb up a neighboring hill to get up close. It was not a trail for the weak of heart, and we were soon climbing down slopes to cross creeks and up the other side. It got steeper and steeper as we progressed, but we were entertained by a group of howler monkeys in the trees. At first I thought the monkeys were throwing things down at us from above, but soon I realized that it was the volcano that was spewing out small rocks which were raining down upon us. Then we began to hear a strange sound, sort of a huffing and puffing, and this was also the volcano announcing an impending eruption. These were all small releases from the cone at the top or vents along the sides, so we were not worried about impending death. At various points you could look out and see Arenal which was barren of any vegetation. Of course, the risk of being hit by a flying rock was greater when you were in the open.

The hike had been exhausting, so the terrace of the hotel was a welcome sight. We sat there that evening and watched the "night show" of lava flowing down the sides of the volcano. This surely would impress even the most jaded tourist.

Our journey home required fording that same river, but we were pros by that time and our confidence was high for a safe crossing. Nearby we enjoyed a brief visit to some hot springs which usually appear near volcanoes, and then we were back in the big city again.

Even though San Jose is a high elevation and does experience seasonal changes, my memory is not good about placing events in proper sequence according to whether it was the rainy, dry, cool or hot season. Mostly the tropics is about the same year round. So I don't remember just when "pejibaya" season happens, but you would never forget the taste, once experienced. This fruit of a palm tree was sold all along the streets and you could smell the pots of water and oil that were boiling the fruit in the background. You would purchase your bag of hot deliciousness and the oil would seep through the paper bag, but it didn't matter. The fruit was easily peeled and the large nut inside removed from the bright orange flesh which, when popped into your mouth, was a culinary delight, tasting something like squash. Even better if you could wait until you got home to add a dollop of mayonnaise. I think the pejibaya was to Costa Rica what sticky rice and mango were to Thailand.

Soon after my arrival, I found the group of women who played mahjong and learned yet another version. Again, there was a mixture of nationalities so a compromise had to be reached about the rules. We played once a week and it was as much about the food being served as playing the game. Every hostess tried to outdo the other, so it was always an adventure for the taste buds.

Another company wife and I had decided that we would take up walking in a nearby park three times a week for exercise. Usually I would drive and park along the side of the busy street which had a boulevard down the center. One day as we were returning along the path from our 45 minute walk, I noticed what appeared to be an accident. The closer we got, the clearer became our view and what at first was someone else's problem became mine. Four vehicles were involved in the mess, two moving cars which had collided and ploughed into my car, pushing it into a truck parked in front of me. The woman who was initially hit pulled me aside to give me the details. A fancy Mercedes had made a U-turn through the boulevard and struck this woman's car, forcing her to hit my car, etc. No one hurt, but the Mercedes man got out, inspected damage to his car and hers and determined there was none, so he suggested to her that they just leave the scene, even though my car was quite damaged back and front. She refused and called the police. When these defenders of the populace arrived, THEY SUGGESTED THE SAME THING! She again refused and made the whole group wait until my friend and I returned from our walk about half an hour later. What a good Samaritan to have stuck to her guns like that even as she faced the police.

Nearing the end of our stay in San Jose, my Thai business partner, Pom, came to stay with us for a while. It was a time that we renewed our long friendship and picked up where we had left off. She eagerly joined the craft classes and began making Victorian sewing boxes for all her friends and family. We also tried something new which was marbleizing. We hauled a large plastic garbage can into my work room, filled it with water and swirled special paint in several colors on the surface. Then we would take clay pots and dip them into the water, picking up the paint in beautiful marble patterns on the surface of the pot. After several pots were dipped, we would take sheets of paper and lay them carefully into the remaining paint on the surface of the water. They would become customized writing paper with matching envelopes. We experimented with many different items, from paper to wood boxes, clay pots and about anything not nailed down, to see what masterpieces would result. If "Life is Supposed to be Fun," we certainly were proving it.

1994–1996

One weekend we decided to take Pom out of the city to see some of the sights, including the Arenal volcano and some spectacular waterfalls. The truck had a double cab, although the back seat was a bit tight. By afternoon a light rain started to fall, which was to be expected there and I began to feel uneasy about how fast Johannes was driving on the wet road. Pom also was sharing this same feeling and we both, in our own ways, said a little prayer for protection. Just in Time! The road made a curve, but the truck suddenly spun out of control and flew off the road, down an embankment and came to rest against a culvert. After taking stock and finding everyone unhurt, we piled out and saw that the truck was also undamaged. Some people from a nearby house came running out and told us that just the previous week a car had also spun out, crashed and killed two people. It seems that there was an oil slick right there on the road and when it rained, it was like a sheet of ice. You would think someone would have thought to clean the oil off the road, no? Having a four wheel drive vehicle proved its worth and we were able to drive right out of that ditch and be on our way. But I still think that there is a lot of power in prayer which kept us all safe that day.

You have heard that "all good things must come to an end?" And so it was. I was teaching yet another craft class that day with a dozen or so women when I got the call. Johannes was on the other end, calling me from Los Angeles where the head office of Dole was now located. He was telling me, with excitement, that we were being transferred back to Davao in the Philippines. He would be the regional director of research for the whole Far East and it was a nice promotion for him. For me, however, that was not my reality. I sank to the floor and burst into tears, much to the consternation of all my students who were thinking that Johannes had come to some horrible end. My thoughts were, oh no, I want our next move to be back to the

San Jose, Costa Rica

United States, not clear over to the other side of the world, and especially not back to Davao. I had spent a lifetime following my husband around the world, however, and, like a good company wife, I would do it again. I extracted a promise from Johannes that this would be our last move, or if he would choose to reassign to yet another place, I would not be going with him. Enough is enough. I began the packing process, sorting everything into two piles, one for storage in the United States and a much smaller pile to bring with us.

Because we had formerly lived in the village of Pandora so many years ago, we were automatically members of an elite group of people who had formed a club and every year they would gather for a party. Some of these people were still employees of Dole, but others had left and found new adventures. But they still remained part of this club. It was decided to make their annual party a farewell party for us, and we would all go in a chartered bus back to Pandora, a journey of several hours. I was excited to be returning to my "starting point" in 1969 and curious as to how it might have changed in these 25 years. After a rowdy ride "down the hill" and into the tropical climate of the eastern coast of Costa Rica, we traveled by road to Pandora which took minutes as compared to the hours by train in our pioneers days.

The company put us all up in guest houses and after I was settled in, I wanted to see my old house at the end of the road. I walked up the same old gravel road, but was barely able to identify which had been my house. Remember the dense forest surrounding three sides, so imposing and impenetrable? Gone. It had all been cleared to make pasture for cows. I almost cried. This was up-in-my-face destruction of the rain forest for the sake of feeding a few cows.

The group had a tour of the plantation and we visited what had been Vesta at the end of the valley and the site of that infamous foot bridge. This farm had been destroyed in an earthquake some years before and the bridge was long gone with it, so there was no danger of having to cross that bridge again.

That evening we had a big party around the community pool with a band and all. Our group and the current Pandora residents attended and the food and fun were flowing. We reminisced about old times and danced into the wee hours. Sleeping that night was easy as the jungle sounds just lulled you into its folds and carried you away.

On our bus ride back up to San Jose, I was sitting next to Jeanne, a woman that I knew only casually but had always wished we had lived in the same place at the same time. Although she did live now in San Jose, she was working and lived on the other side of town, so we never had the opportunity to connect. In talking with her on the bus, I regretted this very much, as now I was leaving and the chance was gone – or so I thought at the time. "Oh ye of little faith!" I was not thinking about how small our world had become.

So our departure from Costa Rica was very bitter sweet. On one hand we had these wonderful memories of great times with wonderful friends, but on the other hand, here we were moving far, far away and chances of ever seeing them again were slim. This was just another fact of life when you worked in the divisions with the company and you had to adjust your mind to accept this tearing apart of relationships every few years.

One good thing about our move was that I was not trying to transport a cat. That in itself was such a relief that the journey was even pleasant. Just another air plane flight half way around the world with only two suitcases. With company personnel

San Jose, Costa Rica

meeting you at every turn along the way and whisking you away in company cars to spend the night in first class hotels, it was not possible to complain about anything. I felt pampered and all I had to do was sit back and think of good things to come.

DAVAO CITY, THE PHILIPPINES
1996–1998

Davao City, the Philippines

Here we were again, touching down in Manila, the ride to the hotel through familiar dirty streets and decrepit buildings, throngs of people in jeepneys (the local transport), on tricycles or pulling carts loaded with merchandise. The traffic, the same quagmire and it took forever as the taxi risked life and limb to make progress. After one night, we were up and away, retracing our hazardous drive to the airport, to catch the early flight which would take us 500 miles south to Davao and our new/old home. The journey seemed endless.

Arriving in Davao was also déjà vu. The terminal was a new building but the rush to claim your bags and head out front to find transportation was the same crush of people. We were met by a company car and chauffeur so our wait was not too long. He whisked us out of the turmoil and down the road a short distance to the hotel where we would be living for the first few months as we, once again, awaited the arrival of all our household goods from the other side of the world.

To anyone coming anew to Davao and staying at this hotel, it would seem a paradise. It is truly a lovely place with a huge garden area at the center and a white sand beach on the Bay of Davao. It is an oasis of tall palms, flowering hibiscus of every color and a koi pond that edges the main lobby. For me, it was a return to a place I did not want to be and my view was clouded by feelings of tiredness and a bit of sadness to be so far away from family and knowing there would be huge chunks of time between visits with no telephone calls in between. But I am a person who does not stay down long and as soon as I had a few days rest from the journey, I began to focus on all the things I needed to accomplish in these first weeks before moving into the house we had chosen while on "look-see." This put me right in the mode of having a <u>project</u> and I charged forward with my list in hand. My spirits began to lift and I felt the old Carol begin to surface.

As soon as I got my car, a brand new silver Mitzubishi Lancer, I headed down to the furniture makers to begin the process of furnishing our house since all of our previous stuff had been put into storage, save a few pieces. I decided to have a set of rattan for the living room, with the idea that in our future we could use it out on a patio. In the twenty years since living here, these factories had become quite sophisticated and now catered almost exclusively to export, producing quality pieces, so I was quite pleased with my choices of design. I chose a nice sofa set with two chairs, two side tables and a coffee table.

The next stop was to go down to the Chinatown of Davao to hunt for a fabric with which to cover the loose cushions on the set. That major street was much the same as before with all the stores selling fabric clumped together in one area. As you would walk along past these stores, there would be all the businesses selling kitchen ware. Then you would begin to see places selling glass and mirrors. Twenty years ago language was a bit of a roadblock because many of the vendors only spoke the local dialect, but this time around everyone spoke English, even the little kids running around. So I think this was some sort of testament to the educational system upgrades that this country had made in those years.

There had been other major changes to the city as well. Now you could go downtown and find a huge mall of stores and large super markets with all manner of products. I was no longer faced with having to open a jar of mayonnaise to see if it was spoiled before buying it. I still went to the open market once a week for produce, and it was still the crowded, smelly, dirty place I remembered from before. But going to an open market had become routine after living all those years in the Third

Davao City, the Philippines

World, and I knew my way around. Another old market where you used to be able to find wonderful antique brass objects was now selling mostly clothing from Indonesia. There was one place still displaying a few antiques, but the prices were so high that I wouldn't even step a foot inside. This was due to the large tourist invasion, many from Japan, and these people would pay any price, so the locals learned quickly to raise their prices. It was true, however, that I was no longer the "collector" that I used to be. You can only acquire so many pieces of brass, baskets or ceramics before every shelf of your house is full and the thrill is gone. It really had to be something special that I couldn't live without before I would put my money down. Or perhaps since I was older and hopefully wiser now, I didn't need all those "things" to make me happy.

At long last our household goods arrived in port and we jumped through all the hoops necessary to get them released and transported to our house. By this time the furniture that I had ordered was ready, so everything came together at about the same time. Our house was in a new subdivision not far from the hotel where we had been staying. In those first few days of getting organized, it was nice to have a bed and shower available to us at the hotel while we were getting settled.

This house had four bedrooms, four baths, large living room and dining room, a generous kitchen which had red tile counter tops, a screened lanai and a huge yard. It was surrounded on four sides with a tall fence which across the front was covered with bouganvillia bushes in all colors. In the huge side yard there was an orchid arbor with well over 100 plants which afforded me fresh cut orchids for the house at all times – a luxury to be sure that I really appreciated.

Then there was the long back wall, two lots in length, on the other side of which was a cock breeding farm. Now this subdivision was all residential and, technically speaking, this sort of operation was not allowed, although a few chickens would have been OK. But this place had 150 cocks, all being bred for fighting, and the owner was some very wealthy man who had paid off the right people, so nothing was done. It didn't take too many days of living in our house to learn something about cocks. They don't just crow as the sun is beginning to arise. No, they go off almost 24 hours a day, all 150 of them! It was a thorn in my side that began to fester quickly. The only relief was to sequester myself in one of our bedrooms and turn on the air conditioning.

The day before moving into the house, I got a call from a local vet who was looking for a baby Siamese kitten for me. She had found one and I should come to pick it up. I asked her to keep it for one day until I had moved into our house, but she could not do that, so I had to bring the kitten back to the hotel to spend the night. I named her Genesis because she was a new beginning. My previous cat, Cheri, had been born in Davao, so Geni was like starting over again. This kitten, however, had not been raised around humans, apparently, and she was terrified. I can tell you, it was an "all-nighter" with her, all the while hoping we were not disturbing neighboring hotel guests. In the morning I took her over to the house and locked her in a back bedroom while some company workers did minor repairs on some windows.

That evening after the workers had gone, I failed to check closely where these workers had been doing their repairs and did not see that they had left one window open. In the morning I awoke and went in search of my new baby and could not find her anywhere. Then as I discovered the open window and looked out, I heard this tiny cry from down below and saw Geni in the bushes. I raced outside, alarming our house guard in

Davao City, the Philippines

the process, and he followed me running around to that side of the house. I suddenly realized that this was going to really spook the kitten, so I stopped the guard and myself in our tracks and explained that I needed to proceed alone, carefully and quietly. And so I rescued my baby whose only damage was that she had picked up a flea.

She soon settled into the house and began to show her true colors. She loved to climb walls, and I mean that literally. A gleam would shine in her eye and she would take off crazy, leap onto some display shelves and zigzag back and forth to the top, then continue up the wall to the ceiling with all the momentum she had built up. She would hang there a few seconds and drop to the floor. I decided that her theme song would be "Wild Thing, I Think I Love You."

But crazy as she was inside the house, she was fearful to be outside. From my bedroom there was a door out to the large side yard, and I would invite her to sit with me out there some mornings. She never left the safety of the steps, however and seemed content to watch birds and bugs from afar. But there was this one day when instinct got the best of her. A flock of birds had the audacity to land right there in the center of the grass and Geni shot off from the stairs like a bullet. When she reached the center of the yard, the birds, of course, easily flew off, and she then realized what she had done. As fast as she had left the safety of the stairs she returned. It was all over in about 10 seconds. I laughed so hard because you could just see the wheels turning in her mind that she wasn't going to do <u>that</u> again any time soon!

Starting anew in a division meant that I had to find myself a new maid. I put the word out and soon had several girls to interview. One made an appointment and never showed up. Another came looking very disheveled. So both were immediately scratched from the list. Then Evelyn showed up, clean, tidy, polite, previous experience. It was a no brainer. Her husband had recently died from tuberculosis and she had two small boys to support. She would live at my house while her kids stayed with a relative. I liked her immediately and we settled into a good working relationship.

But several months into our stay, Evelyn became sick and it was diagnosed that she also had tuberculosis. This is a disease that is endemic in the Philippines, and since she was in such close proximity to someone who had it, she was almost certain to contract the disease sooner or later. We got her started on the medical program that the government runs and she went back home for several months until she was stabilized. In the meantime, I also consulted with a doctor about our personal risk and was informed that it was probably very low. I put worry aside, having much better things to do with my time and thoughts.

There were plenty of opportunities to fill the days. Never a dull moment if you just asked around. I found the mahjong group and began my weekly session. And there were several charity groups to choose from. I became acquainted with the group of women who were helping a local nun who was running a rehab clinic for people with disabilities. She had a workshop which was making artificial limbs for amputees and was installing some very sophisticated computer equipment which would revolutionize the process. Also she was running a community home for families of these disabled people while they recuperated. So it all needed lots of money and I decided it was a very worthy cause.

I jumped right in with all my craft ideas which could be sold in bazaars held a couple times a year. There were Victorian sewing boxes and stuffed animals to be made, and I even began

Davao City, the Philippines

to make mirrors with stained glass overlays. There was one large piece which I made that was a prize at a raffle. A large stuffed dragon, made with satin in rainbow colors, was also auctioned off.

But the stuffed rabbits really took off in popularity. I found a shop down in Chinatown selling fake fur and began to make large rabbits which were dressed as a boy or girl. Of course, I put Evelyn to work making them also, which she really enjoyed. Orders began to come in from ladies in the community and I would give Evelyn a little money for her work and the rest would go to the nun and her clinic.

By the end of my stay in Davao, about two years, I had lumped together a nice sum of money which was going to buy a new commercial oven for one of the nun's projects. This adventure was to bake small cakes to be sold in the community, thus employing a bunch of people and with the idea of expanding to grander things in the future.

About one year after we had returned to Davao, Johannes came home and said, "You will never believe who walked into my office today." Of course, I could not even begin to imagine, and waited patiently for him to tell me or at least give me a clue. At last he released me from the agonizing wait and said it was Fico Odio, the husband of Jeanne who was the Costa Rican woman whom I had regretted not getting to know better in San Jose. They were being transferred by their company to Davao. Like us, twenty years before, they had lived here at the same time as us, but at that time Jeanne had small children and she "ran" in other circles than I did. So here they would be joining us again, and now was my opportunity to get to know Jeanne after all those years.

When Jeanne arrived we began a friendship as if we had known each other well for 20 years. It was one of those things that just clicked immediately. And it came at a time that I really needed a good friend. She joined me in the rabbit making adventure and, being the generous to a fault person that she was, jumped with every ounce of her being into charity work.

At this time, Jeanne was about to become a new grandmother, a prospect that excited her to no end. I don't believe I have ever known a woman who was so "in" to babies. So I introduced Jeanne to English smocking, since I had a small machine that does the pleating and had learned this embroidery technique some years previous. We began to make baby clothes for this new grandchild and made many trips to Chinatown to hunt for wonderful fabrics. Our behavior could only be described as obsessive as we made dresses, sleep ware, dresses, rompers and more dresses. By the time she went back to Costa Rica to meet her new grandchild, she had a whole suitcase full of precious outfits. I do believe that doing all that smocking saved her sanity while she awaited the happy day.

Coming from a musical family, I was always interested to participate in singing. The first time around in Davao I had joined a community choir which was performing the Messiah one Christmas, and this time around I happened upon another choir that was practicing for a similar event. I don't claim to have a very good voice, but I can read music and carry a tune. This qualified me to participate and I was eager to be part of it.

Before our big event, we were going to perform at a smaller event, sort of as a dress rehearsal. A school was having an evening musical event and we would be performing up on a raised stage set up on the outdoor basketball court. We spent the previous day decorating some tall folding screens that would serve as the backdrop for our group, covering them with black cloth and attaching silver stars all over.

Davao City, the Philippines

We endured a long program of children singing their hearts out, off key but with enthusiasm, and finally our group was to perform the finale. We would sing one song from the Messiah and then would sing the Irish Blessing. By this time of the evening we could see that a storm was brewing and a light wind began to blow. We were hoping to finish before the rain began, but as we launched into our final song, things began to go south. The words of the Irish Blessing begin, "May the road rise up to greet you and the wind be always at your back," or something to that effect. At <u>precisely</u> that moment a huge gust of wind did rise up and blew the whole backdrop over upon us. We all began to laugh at the coincidence and scrambled to rebuild our backdrop. But the show must go on, and we regrouped to finish the program. What troupers we all were!

I was curious to make a return trip to Picnic Island, the place our group of families would boat out to on a Sunday morning to spend the day snorkeling and hanging out on the disserted beach. At last the opportunity arose to see what had happened in the twenty years since. The island was now private and had been turned into a luxury resort, first class all the way. Now lounging would be done around a lovely pool surrounded by lush gardens. You could rent a cabana to spend the night also and enjoy a wonderful meal at the restaurant. Tourism was alive and well, but I sort of missed the primitive, pristine beach of the past. There was something about getting all sticky with salt, sand coating your legs and the exhaustion at the end of the day that made you feel almost virtuous.

I took the opportunity to become more computer savvy by signing up for a course being offered downtown. It meant several trips a week to a small building and climbing a steep flight of stairs to get to the class. All the instructions were given on the computer and you just followed along at your own pace with an instructor nearby for any problems in understanding. Upon finishing the course, I don't think I learned much that I could apply practicably, but it probably was a good exercise for my brain, and I surely needed that.

During these years Johannes and I had been looking around for a good place to retire. He was getting close to that age and it was good to have some sort of plan in place. Sometimes while on vacation we would take side trips to retirement communities we had read about in various countries, and sometimes we specifically went to a place where we had heard lots of Americans were retiring. We had crossed Costa Rica off the list first because of the high crime in that country, the drug business having moved north from Colombia. Next we went to Guadalajara in Mexico to have a look, but that seemed way too "Third World" for me. Then there was Bend, Oregon, which was highly reputed to be great, but looked nothing special to us. South Carolina was pretty and stayed on our list of possibilities.

Toward the end, we had pretty much settled on the idea of living in the United States, and I was very happy with that. It couldn't come soon enough for me, but Johannes' plan was, "When I am 60 years old, have 30 years of work with the company, and the year 2000, I will retire." I think he liked all those zeros. And thus it was written in stone. I felt as if I were treading water for that time to arrive.

After this next event, I was literally champing at the bit to get back to the States. As related earlier, on the other side of our back wall was this cock breeding business which I was coping with fairly well. That is until "the gong" incident. Johannes was away on one trip or another and I was alone except for the night guard who stayed outside in our carport. Suddenly I was awakened in the night, sitting bolt upright in the

Davao City, the Philippines

bed, with the sound of a piece of metal striking another piece of metal, a huge "kabong." It was so loud that I could feel the vibration in my bones. I got out of bed and looked through all my windows around the house but could see nothing. After many strikes it suddenly quit. I relaxed and went back to sleep, only to be jolted awake again by a single strike. Again after a short while, I was asleep. By the third and fourth time, I realized that this very disturbing sound was happening on the hour, each strike one more than the last. Finally morning arrived and I went out to talk with the guard. He had also heard the noise, had walked around the yard to investigate and found nothing. But he had determined that the noise was coming from the cock farm.

The next night the same thing happened, and I knew this had to stop. Surely I was not the only one in the neighborhood who was upset. I decided to take with me my daytime guard, a woman named Helen, and we would go over to that farm to protest. When we arrived, I began to call out for the guard or anyone, but there was no answer. So I thought I had the right to enter the property, all the while calling out for anyone there because I needed to resolve this issue then and there. Helen was extremely nervous and would not come with me as I walked around the property. Then I saw "IT," a large 4" metal pipe hanging in a tree with a smaller pipe tucked into the crotch of the trunk. Now what to do? I knew I needed to make my presence known, but also knew that I did not DARE steal the dastardly thing. So I decided to untie the large pipe and lay it on the ground. This would at least signal that someone had been there. My next step was to contact our company office to get some authoritative help. I needed some weight behind me. They contacted the owner and, thank God, I never heard the gong again. I learned that the reason it had been put into place was to keep the guards awake during the night by ringing it every hour! What about the neighbors who wanted to sleep?

I was having just about enough of this Third World stuff. I was tired of being that "good company wife" and I felt it was my turn to begin living the life that I wanted. I really wanted to move into the Twenty First Century before I was too old and I was beginning to make this known to my husband. Now I don't think I ever voiced this in a nagging way, but just let him know where I stood on the issue.

On what was to be our last vacation back to the States, we passed by Las Vegas, which was our usual first stop to get over jet lag, and after spending several days down on The Strip at a hotel there, we went to visit my best friend Carole who had moved to Vegas after her recent divorce. It was late August, the hottest time of the year there, but Johannes enjoyed walking in her community built around five lakes, and in the evening would sit on a bench down by the lake, soaking in the view of the mountains in the distance. Who knew that there was this quiet, beautiful city beyond the casinos?

Johannes left to return to Davao and I stayed on with my friend for two weeks, just enjoying our reunion after such a long time. It was during this time that I decided that Las Vegas was the place to which we should retire. It had everything on the list of things we wanted, even an international airport close by. To this end, Carole and I began to "plant the seed" in the mind of the universe. I found a gorgeous tall urn that I needed to have but which I, of course, could not fit into my suitcase, so I left it with Carole, to be picked up whenever the day arrived for our return to the States. While I was there, we placed our wishes into that urn, mentally, and after I left, Carole continued daily to place thoughts of my return into that urn. Some of you may not think there is any power in such an undertaking, but just think of it as the power of prayer.

Davao City, the Philippines

At last my two weeks were up and I needed to return to Davao. I brought back with me a lovely panoramic photograph of the lakes and mountains behind, and I placed it on my refrigerator. Each morning I would give it a kiss and say, "See you soon." What with Carole working on her end and me on mine, Johannes did not stand a chance. It took only THREE DAYS of this "woo-woo" to bring about our desire. Johannes was up in Manila and gave me a call, telling me that he had quit his job! I almost fainted. Could it be true? After all, wasn't it written in stone that he wouldn't retire until 2000? This was only 1998. When he arrived home we began to discuss where we would go and I suggested Las Vegas. He said sure, and that was that. It took all of 30 seconds to make the decision. Now it was a matter of Johannes tying up ends at work.

I began to wonder just how long it would take to get the signal to start packing, and it was difficult for me to face what could take months. So I suggested that I pack the house and go on ahead. I could look for a house, buy a car, and get settled and he could come when he was ready. This plan was agreed upon and the move began.

First we sold my car and set up a bank account for Evelyn who would use the money to attend the university, studying hotel and restaurant management. We hoped this would give her a leg up for her future.

Within the next two weeks I had completed the packing and had my one-way ticket in hand. I just needed to take the cat to the vet for her shots so she could travel on the plane and enter the States.

There were the usual farewell parties to attend, but this was one move where I had no regrets about leaving. I was going home at last and it was one of the happiest times of my life.

EPILOGUE

The last chapter has been written of a book which I never imagined, in my wildest dreams, would happen. I know my mother is looking down with a huge smile and saying, "There, I knew you could do it." Actually writing these stories has proved to be such an easy effort that I am wondering if perhaps she didn't have a hand in it after all. If you have ever told stories of your life, I would encourage you to write them down for your family. Spell check will help immensely for those of you who, like myself, can't spell their way out of a paper bag. It is such a rewarding task, and, in my case, will enlighten my family of the 30 years spent living a life distant and different from theirs in so many ways.

So now here I am back in the good ol' U.S.A. Would I ask for the same life in a do over? In a heartbeat, even with all the lizards, snakes, spiders and hassles. The rewards have been far too numerous to list, not to mention the huge lessons learned in appreciation of the small things in life. One example I will give you is in the first few weeks of my return, I would go into a supermarket looking, lets say, for Ziplock bags. My first impulse would be to buy five or six boxes, and I would have to pinch myself and remember that the supermarket was only a few blocks away from my new house and I did not have to buy a year's worth of anything any more. What a marvelous feeling of freedom that was.

My dreams of world travel all came true and I am left with a collection of beautiful memories that will fill me to my end. Now, instead of having to retell my stories, however, I can just say, "Hey, I have written a book about this and you can buy it."

ABOUT THE AUTHOR

Carol Eve (Wollangk) Klink was born the third of five children in the small town of Omro, Wisconsin. She graduated from Kaukauna High School in 1960 and attended the University of Wisconsin from 1964 through 1967 with a major in Related Art, Interior Design. In 1968 she married Johannes W. Klink from Emmelord, Holland, and they resided in Manhattan, Kansas, for six months before he accepted a position with Standard Fruit Company (now Dole Foods Company) in Costa Rica.

They spent the next 30 years living abroad in various countries and, since retiring in 1998, they have lived in Las Vegas, Nevada.

www.ingramcontent.com/pod-product-compliance
Lightning Source LLC
Chambersburg PA
CBHW071706090426
42738CB00009B/1687